EARTHQUAKE
PREDICTION

HAROUN

TAZIEFF

EARTHQUAKE

PREDICTION

McGraw-Hill, Inc.

New York St. Louis San Francisco Auckland Bogotá
Caracas Hamburg Lisbon London Madrid
Mexico Milan Montreal New Delhi Paris
San Juan São Paulo Singapore
Sydney Tokyo Toronto

English Language Edition

Translated by Nicholas Hartmann
in collaboration with
The Language Service, Inc.
Poughkeepsie, New York

Typography by AB Typesetting
Poughkeepsie, New York

Library of Congress Cataloging-in-Publication Data

Tazieff, Haroun, 1914–
   [*Prévision des séismes*. English]
   Earthquake prediction/Haroun Tazieff.
      p. cm. — (The McGraw-Hill *HORIZONS OF SCIENCE* series)
   Translation of: *Prévision des séismes*.
   Includes bibliographical references.
   ISBN 0-07-062992-7
   1. Earthquake prediction. 2. Earthquake engineering.
3. Disaster relief. I. Title. II. Series.
QE538.8.T3913 1992
551.2'2—dc20   91-33149

The original French language edition of this book
was published as *La Prévision des séimes* copyright © 1989,
Hachette: Paris, France.
Questions de science series
Series editor: Dominique Lecourt

TABLE OF CONTENTS

INTRODUCTION

From time immemorial, human beings have feared earthquakes as the ineluctable and overpowering messengers of Doom.

Homer, like Hesiod, believed that they expressed the terrible rage of Poseidon, god of the sea and the true prince of cataclysms. The Chinese discerned in them the tremblings and convulsions of the Great Dragon who they believed lived in the bowels of the Earth and shook the mountains and plains when irritated. The Japanese were convinced that Earth tremors were the furious contortions of Namazu, the giant catfish who dwelt in the ooze.

It will no doubt surprise the reader to learn that, despite the destructive power and emotional impact of these phenomena, it was not until the mid-20th century that a definitive and rational understanding was gained of what the previous century had begun to call "seisms." Of course terror is not conducive to knowledge; in fact it nourishes superstition, which in turn precludes understanding.

Thales, the founder of the School of Miletus in Ionia in the 6th century B.C., was already aware of that. A pioneer of Greek science, his ambition was to provide natural explanations for natural phenomena; in a celebrated adage, he deplored the fact that everything was "full of gods." Taking up the thread of ancient Egyptian and Babylonian myths, he theorized that the Earth was

supported by water, and proceeded to explain earthquakes as the agitation of that water on which it floated.
He thus did his utmost to give the irascible Poseidon his
walking papers.

But it was the late 4th-century B.C. Greek philoso-
pher Epicurus who, convinced that physical knowledge
would deliver humankind from irrational fears and confer
on his fellow-citizens the most perfect spiritual tranquil-
lity, sketched out the first explanation in any detail of the
mechanism that controlled Earth tremors. It comes in the
famous *Letter to Pythocles* which, having discussed climate changes, the formation of clouds, the nature of
thunder, lightning, and the thunderbolt, and the genesis of
cyclones, goes on to address the serious question of the
origin of earthquakes.

He believed it was possible to discern their cause in
the wind "imprisoned" within the Earth, "which comes
both from outside, and from the fact that as the strata
located above subterranean caves collapse, the air which is
compressed therein is transformed into wind." Epicurus,
like most ancient authors who espoused some sort of cav-
ern myth, believed that the Earth's interior was riddled
with caves, grottos, and crevices. This is why, alongside his
first explanation, he can advance another purely mechanical one: "Earthquakes can also result from propagation of
the movement caused by the collapse of a considerable
mass of terrestrial strata, and by the rebound which it expe-
riences when it strikes objects more dense than itself."

Lucretius (99–ca. 55 B.C.), in book VI of his admirable poem *De rerum natura* [On the nature of things],

picks up these hypotheses, enriches them, and enhances their ethical value. Recalling the disaster which overthrew the city of Sidon near Tyre, and the one that destroyed the island of Aegina between Attica and the Peloponnesos, the great poet gave voice to the fright which seizes the populace when a "shudder" makes everything tremble: "Then through the towns runs a two-headed terror: fear that the roofs will collapse, and fear that the subterranean caves will be destroyed, that—as the Earth is rent asunder—Nature will open up a vast abyss and fill it with a jumbled mass of ruins."

With this same intention of "pacifying the soul" but in a Stoic vein, Seneca (ca. 4 B.C.– 65 A.D) (who remembered the earthquake that devastated Campania in 63 A.D.), devoted several pages of his *Quaestiones naturales* [Investigations in natural science] to a meditation on the terror which people experience when faced with the earthquakes, so frequent and so violent, that rock the Mediterranean basin. He invites humankind to liberate itself from this fear not simply by looking Death in the eye, but by understanding the causes of these formidable phenomena.

Seneca recalls the teachings of Posidonius of Apamea (ca. 135 – ca. 51 B.C.), and mentions the descriptions that he gives. He identifies two types of violent Earth movements: the *succusio*, in which the Earth is shaken vertically; and the more dangerous *inclinatio*, which makes it oscillate first to one side and then to the other, like a ship. He also adds the simple vibration of objects.

9

But there is more to earthquakes than just their emotional impact. They cannot be explained without a theory of the Earth's internal structure, which leads directly to the prickly question of our planet's history. With the waning of antiquity, this question would for centuries be a forbidden subject, since it was assumed to have been definitively settled by Scripture.

It was Descartes (1595–1650), taking infinite precautions in terms of form but demonstrating a radical boldness in his subject matter, who dared to write in 1644, in his *Principia philosophiae* [Principles of philosophy], that "this Earth where we live was once a heavenly body no different from the Sun, except that it was smaller." Resorting to the fiction of a fable within a fable, he "sidesteps" the Bible and, for the first time, considers the history of the world and the arrangement of its parts in terms of mechanics. For him, the center of the Earth is still molten and in the process of cooling. In this way he ends up proposing a new explanation for the origin of earthquakes, namely as dislocations of the "terrestrial vault."

"In addition to the vapors which rise from the waters," he explains, "there also emerges from the Earth's interior a great quantity of penetrating and corrosive spirits, and several fatty and oily exhalations." But when these exhalations are "too agitated thus to be converted into oil and meet underground in fissures and concavities which previously contained only air, they form a thick and oily smoke which may be compared to that of a candle when it has just been extinguished. And just as the latter readily flares up as soon as the flame of another candle is brought near, thus when some spark is struck in these concavities, it will spread incontinently throughout the smoke with which they are filled and thereby the material of the smoke, transformed into flame, suddenly becomes rarefied and presses, with great violence, on all sides of the place within which it is confined." This, concludes Descartes, "is how earthquakes arise."

During that same period the Reverend Father Athanasius Kircher (1601–1680), who in 1638 had observed an eruption of Vesuvius accompanied by an earthquake, had constructed a "theoretical system of the subterranean fires of which volcanoes are the vents." His *Mundus subterraneus* [The underground world], published in 1664, also suggests that the Earth (like the Sun) is a heavenly body that is still evolving. Another contemporary, the great English physicist and chemist Robert Hooke (1635–1703), noted in his description of earthquakes in 1668 that they caused boulders to be uplifted, and saw in this one of the causes of mountain-building.

There can be no doubt that these books prepared the way for the science of geology, but its actual foundation undoubtedly dates from the works of Niels Stensen, called Steno, of Denmark (1638–1686), a friend of Spinoza and later of Leibniz, a frail and brilliant anatomist who turned to the study of fossils and wrote, before taking Holy Orders, an incomparable geological history of Tuscany commissioned by Grand Duke Ferdinand II of Florence. But it is obvious that the study of earthquakes had lost any inherent appeal: in most cases they were explained only as an argument illustrating some general doctrine of Earth history in a context marked by theological squabbles. The immediate objective, the urgent concern of the Ancients had been lost sight of: no longer was the purpose to deliver people from the anxiety which grips them. Instead, we find discussions of the Old Testament. Is it because the philosophers of that era had only a remote relationship to earthquakes, since most of them lived in a geographical area where tremors are relatively rare and, aside from some well-known exceptions, not very destructive? Is it because the ancient idea of Doom had retreated before the concept of Providence?

So it was, when a major disaster struck the city of Lisbon on November 1, 1755, and reawakened the old terror, that precious few explanations were offered. Despite the appearance six years earlier of Buffon's *Théorie de la Terre* [Theory of Earth]; not much more was known then about the causes of earthquakes than had been known a few centuries earlier. It was the philosophers who appropriated the event: Voltaire invoked it as a decisive argument in the debate which pitted him against the optimism of Leibniz:

> *All is good, you say, and all is necessary;*
> *What! Would the whole universe have been worse off*
> *Without that infernal chasm, without engulfing Lisbon?*

It has been said that the 19th century represented the Golden Age of the development of Earth sciences, since not only geology itself but also prehistory, mineralogy, petrography, and paleontology began to flourish then. It was the age of the first great modern scientific expeditions, when exploration began on an international scale. In the United States, petroleum exploration began in 1859. Economic, financial, and political powers focused their intense attention on this area of research.

That century also witnessed the appearance of grand theoretical syntheses which demolished old ideas about the structure and evolution of our planet: from Charles Lyell's *Principles of Geology* between 1830 and 1833 from which Darwin drew so many questions and suggestions for the *Origin of Species*—to the monumental *Cosmos* of Alexander von Humboldt (1769–1859), which embodied the century's collected wisdom concerning the physical constitution of the universe. Geological maps proliferated, and the teaching of Earth sciences, which Joseph de Maistre had so recently considered a satanic subject, became established in universities around the world.

But it was only with the invention of the seismograph at the very end of the century that knowledge of the Earth's internal structure really progressed, and a systematic understanding of earthquakes became a possibility.

Reuben Paschwitz, using the pendulum as a model, is often credited with the invention of this instrument which can record the waves generated by seismic activity. Since these waves can propagate thousands of miles from the epicenter—the point on the Earth's surface directly above the earthquake's focus—it was now possible to study earthquakes from a distance, simply by deciphering the resulting "seismograms" to analyze the shape, identity, and sequence of the waves.

This new instrument may be considered a distant descendant of the "earthquake weather vane" invented by the Chinese mathematician Chang Hang in 132 A.D. The seismograph was very soon perfected by the English mining engineer John Milne (1850–1913) and Prince Boris Golitsyn (1862–1916) in Russia, then by Robert Wood (1868–1955) and 1977 Nobel Prize laureate Philip W. Anderson (b. 1923) in the United States. But seismology as such would never have seen the light of day without the work of scholars such as 1904 Nobel Prize laureate John William Strutt, 3rd Baron Rayleigh (1842–1919), Augustus Edward Love (1863–1940) and Charles Francis Richter (1900–1985), who incorporated seismic observations into the framework of a theory of earthquake wave propagation. In Japan, naturally partial to such research, a remarkable school of seismology had been established at the end of the century, and in 1892, following the Mino-Owari earthquake a year earlier, the Imperial Diet set up a special scientific commission that gave a sort of official blessing to the discipline.

But it was the need to monitor underground nuclear tests, beginning in the 1950s, that gave the decisive impetus to this research. Sixty Western countries quickly joined forces in a global network of seismological stations that have since accumulated an impressive amount of data about our planet's seismic activity, which has proved to be much more intense and continuous than had been realized.

Many mysteries would have remained unsolved, especially the question of why seismically active zones are distributed as they are, if these observations and their interpretations had not been fitted into a general theory that everyone now knows as "plate tectonics," which integrates the great geophysical and geological phenomena—earthquakes, volcanoes, mountain-building, etc.—into a coherent whole.

The history behind the creation of this theory is itself very instructive. Largely the work of the Canadian J. Tuzo Wilson, it did not become accepted in the scientific world until the late 1960s. Its essential thesis is that the thin crust covering the Earth is made up of enormous plates assembled into a gigantic mosaic; these plates are not fixed, but move over the spherical surface of the "mantle" of liquid magma in which their bases are immersed.

This theory confirms, with certain additions and corrections, the hypothesis of "continental drift" advanced in 1910 by Alfred Lothar Wegener (b. 1880). But the response to this hypothesis cannot even be described as skeptical: his ideas were met with brutal rejection and systematic denigration. Highly respected as an explorer (he died in 1930 on an expedition to Greenland), this "Viking of science," as he has been called, had the insolence to be a meteorologist, and to advance a revolutionary hypothesis in a field reserved for geophysicists!

Yet another impertinence: his hypothesis, developed in 1915 in a masterpiece entitled *Die Entstehung der Kontinente und Ozeane* [The origin of the continents and oceans], was apparently based on a speculative idea suggested by the outline of the Atlantic Ocean. Picking up on previous observations, especially those made by a certain Antonio Snider (1858) and then more recently by the

Americans W.H. Pickering, H.B. Baker, and F.B. Taylor, Wegener postulated that Africa and South America had once been united in a single continent: the "fit" between their coastlines appeared almost perfect from a distance, as a glance at any map will confirm. Having accumulated more observations, he ultimately presented a very tightly reasoned hypothesis stating that these two continents had moved away from each other over the eons.

Wegener freely admitted, as late as 1929, that he was unable to explain the motive force behind these continental shifts; however he made the most of the extraordinary fertility of his hypothesis. It had shed new light on the present and past distribution of plants and animals, especially on the astonishing resemblances between South American and African fossils; previous ideas about climate change and the causes of the Ice Ages were overturned. However, when a major conference on the subject was organized in New York in 1926, most of the geologists in attendance covered Wegener with scorn. "Fairy tales!" was their verdict. For forty years the hypothesis was almost never again taken seriously.

The theory of "plate tectonics" has now irrefutably established that this meteorologist from Berlin was right. Applying the idea of "drift" not just to continents but to larger "plates" which also include the ocean floor, it has answered the question of displacement forces that had defeated Wegener.

It might therefore seem that we now have at our disposal all the scientific information needed to predict earthquakes. We would thus finally be in a position to make the Ancients' dream come true: to allay for all time our fear of the massive destruction that they cause. This achievement would be even more significant now that—as a result of demographic expansion and especially of the conditions under which urbanization has occurred, particularly in the Third World—earthquakes are much more deadly than they were in antiquity.

But the word "prediction" is clouded with uncertainty, since although geophysics and seismology allow us to "predict" the regions in which most earthquakes will occur and to determine those areas that are most at risk, we are still unable to identify the exact place, the date, or even the intensity of the next earthquake in any given region. It is this precision, however, that is important if we want to "predict" not merely for the sake of foreseeing, but as a means of anticipating by taking precautions: in other words to apply a policy of prevention in order to save human lives.

Is this incapability permanent? It would seem so, since these disciplines operate on geological time scales which rule out any comprehension of individual events. Must we then resign ourselves to knowledge without power? Certainly we must if we continue to demand of such knowledge the power to do something which it cannot do, and which in any event we have no right to ask of it.

But a new method has just emerged, and from a completely different direction: that of empirical research on earthquake precursor signals. Developed by three physicists as a way to deal with the repeated catastrophes which continue to shake Greece, its name is an acronym of the names of its creators: VAN.

Haroun Tazieff takes up the cause of this theory, presenting its principles and demonstrating its successes. He explains the few failures that it has suffered. He refutes the arguments of its opponents, invoking the ghost of Wegener. He acknowledges that it does not (yet?) fit in with existing geophysical theories. No matter: since it exists and it works, he believes that failing to implement it would be criminal. He suggests incorporating it into a prevention system that has been recast in new terms, and denounces the universally and scandalously negligent attitude of public officials in this regard.

Haroun Tazieff does not mince words: he spares neither the experts nor the politicians. Based on his experience, as a field researcher all over the world and then as a government official, he accuses. And, with his much acclaimed ardor and spirit, he proposes solutions. Readers will find all of his arguments here, and will be able to judge for themselves. They will see how in our time, on this particularly "hot" issue, certain questions of science are intimately bound up with questions of politics and ethics.

Dominique LECOURT

MAPS

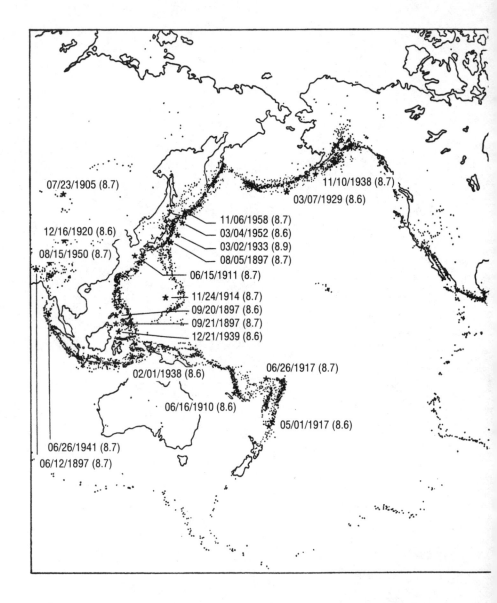

07/23/1905 (8.7)

11/10/1938 (8.7)
03/07/1929 (8.6)

12/16/1920 (8.6)

11/06/1958 (8.7)
03/04/1952 (8.6)
03/02/1933 (8.9)
08/05/1897 (8.7)

08/15/1950 (8.7)

06/15/1911 (8.7)

11/24/1914 (8.7)
09/20/1897 (8.6)
09/21/1897 (8.7)
12/21/1939 (8.6)

06/26/1917 (8.7)

02/01/1938 (8.6)

06/16/1910 (8.6)

05/01/1917 (8.6)

06/26/1941 (8.7)
06/12/1897 (8.7)

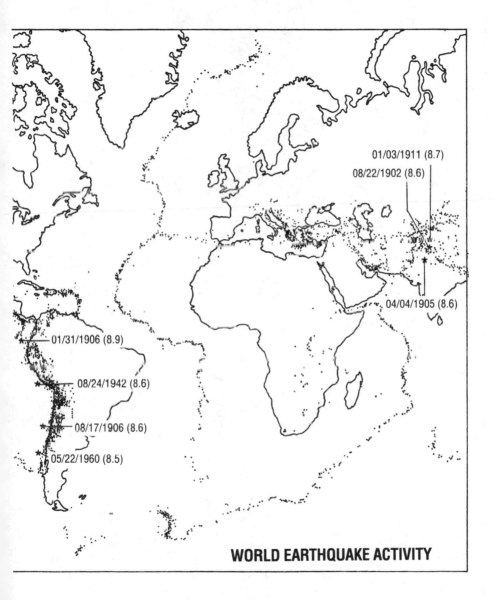

01/03/1911 (8.7)
08/22/1902 (8.6)

04/04/1905 (8.6)

01/31/1906 (8.9)

08/24/1942 (8.6)

08/17/1906 (8.6)

05/22/1960 (8.5)

WORLD EARTHQUAKE ACTIVITY

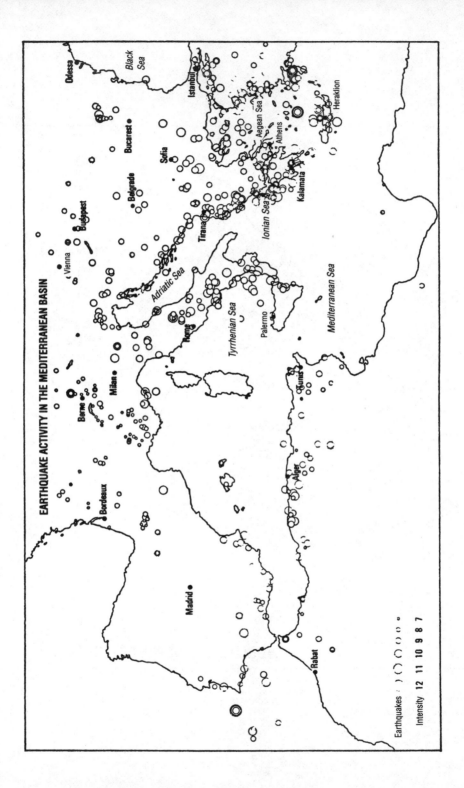

EARTHQUAKE ACTIVITY IN THE MEDITERRANEAN BASIN

Earthquakes :
Intensity 12 11 10 9 8 7

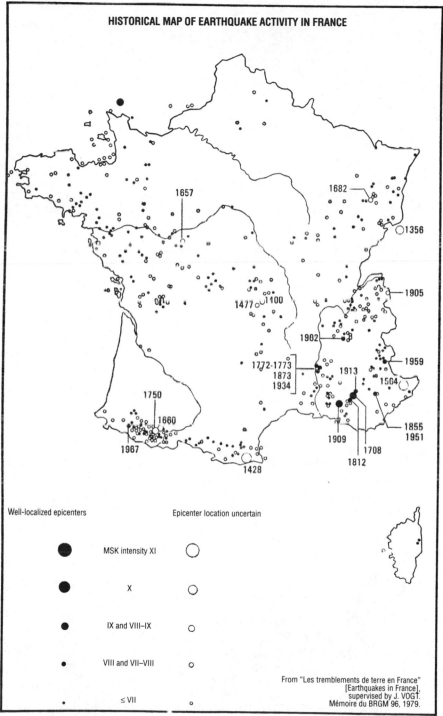

HISTORICAL MAP OF EARTHQUAKE ACTIVITY IN FRANCE

Well-localized epicenters

Epicenter location uncertain

MSK intensity XI

X

IX and VIII–IX

VIII and VII–VIII

≤ VII

From "Les tremblements de terre en France"
[Earthquakes in France],
supervised by J. VOGT.
Mémoire du BRGM 96, 1979.

I

THE SEISMIC RISK:

J'ACCUSE

My intention is not to write some review, or summary, in the acceptably neutral manner of academic literature, about the state of a science (seismology) that is not my specialty. I am concerned with the effects of earthquakes and with ways of protecting the population from them, and not with the study of seismic waves. This subject has fascinated me for more than thirty years. It is too serious for mere academic discourse. It is the battleground for intense interactions involving science, technology, and sociology, and marked by the pressing interests and ambitions (acknowledged or otherwise) of persons, parties, or groups which exist for profit.

So whether you are one of the innumerable potential victims of an earthquake, or someone responsible for protecting the public, you, the reader, must not only understand the basics of what science and technology have to say about various aspects of this complex problem, but you must also, and most importantly, be informed about what is seldom or never talked about: the economic, social, political, and—far too often—personal factors which make protection so much less effective than it could be. Enough of the "code of silence": let us bluntly say what must be said about the administrative, deontological, and ethical shortcomings of those "in charge," whom the citizenry have voted into "decision-making" office, whether directly (as politicians), or indirectly (as civil servants).

My only purpose here is to help open the eyes of concerned people to reality, so they can exercise their rights as citizens in order to improve an intolerable situation. If we do not act more quickly, the next earthquake will kill 10 to 100 times more people than if we had decided, finally, to make some effort to predict earthquakes, to build earthquake-resistant structures, to educate the public, and to prepare and organize relief services so they are effective.

We have the immense good fortune to live in a democracy. But what does that good fortune mean if not, above all, the freedom to tell the truth? And especially to tell the truth when it displeases the decision-makers. It also means the freedom to choose one's elected officials, in other words to choose the "princes who govern us," or are supposed to govern us, or imagine that they do.

But democracy has real value only if voters possess the minimal knowledge which allows them to vote with some understanding. If they do not, they are nothing but an ignorant herd whose votes are conditioned by the prejudices which some propaganda, some media, some party, pressure group, or religion has managed to impose on them. The practice of democracy lives up to its theory only if citizens take an interest in the running of their republic, not just during election campaigns when flattery and false promises fill the air, but during the entire term of the mandate granted to their various elected officials. This applies to every facet of social life. Public safety is one of those facets, and not the least important. Every citizen should be sufficiently well-informed to choose his or her elected officials so as to maximize that safety, and to insist that it be continually improved as those officials perform their duties.

Acquiring that knowledge, which I hope every voter will be able to gain, requires intelligible information. But most information on this subject is far from clear. The reason is that those who are (theoretically) responsible for prevention do not want anyone to know that such information is practically nonexistent. But that fact is obvious, since too many of those in positions of responsibility are themselves ignorant about the subject and, what is worse, prefer to remain that way. For example, since major earthquakes are extremely rare in France—there are between two and half a dozen every century—they prefer not to think about them, hoping that they will never occur again. Their ignorance of history and geology sustains them in the illusion that at least there might not be another one until their term of office is over.

What is more, there are too many "people in charge" who lack the courage to speak certain truths which might displease those on whom their careers depend. This failure is of course at the root of the now-famous "no comment" style of language which characterizes our age, in public life and the universities, among politicians and among scientists. It prevents society from making progress and, where public safety is concerned, keeps it from rising to a level commensurate with our current scientific and technical understanding.

I want us to end up protecting ourselves as best we can against the risk of seismic catastrophe. To do so, we must recall not only some facts, but some truths that are too often (and deliberately) concealed. These truths, as we shall see, have more to do with people than with technology. For example, what about the people we call "experts"?

EXPERTS

The word "expert," at least when used in the context of matters more consequential than the authenticity of a work of art or a rare postage stamp, cloaks in a mantle of respectability certain persons called upon to give an opinion, *a priori* definitive and restrictive, on subjects which concern people's health or their lives, not to mention their property or their well-being. Now I have learned from experience, confirmed time and time again, that real experts—those worthy of the respect supposedly their due—are in fact the exception. Why? Because in order to earn that title, they must meet three criteria, and if a single one is absent the status of "expert" cannot be granted.

The first of these conditions is true expertise. All too often experts have hardly any, and they may turn out to have none at all; one such acid test came on the occasion of the eruption of La Soufrière on the island of Guadeloupe in 1976. The second condition is that real experts must prove themselves to be not only incorruptible but also immune to pressure from those around them; this may seem self-evident, but it is not always the case. The third condition demands of true expert the courage to express their opinions, even when those opinions displease their peers or the powers that be, and thus jeopardize their own careers.

Real experts, who meet these three *sine qua non* conditions, are rather rare.

It has been eighty years since France has experienced a seriously destructive killer earthquake. That means that the next one or ones cannot be far off. Too little has been done, however, to diminish the predictable consequences. That fact can be explained by an almost universal ignorance, prior to the 1980s, of the reality of the danger and the means of reducing it; but there are many unstated reasons for it as well. Most of them have to do with some people's vanity, with other people's inadequate sense of public service, with purely political motives, with egotistical corporations, and with professional jealousies—in the microcosms of both academia and government.

I believe it is absolutely necessary to speak these unpleasant truths in order to define and then implement measures which will reduce the catastrophic consequences of the earthquake which, I repeat, is almost certain to strike France soon. I believe it is almost as important to understand this sorry situation as it is to explain what earthquakes are, what efforts are being made to predict them, and how we can defend ourselves against them.

SCIENCE AND GOVERNMENT

Today more than yesterday, and tomorrow more so than today, the political leaders of a country need and will need the advice of competent scientists, whether this involves, as it does in this case, mitigating the effects of natural disasters, or selecting some technology that is not only expensive but critical to an entire sector of the national economy. When the chemical industry, metallurgy, national defense, meteorology, mineral prospecting, public health, telecommunications, or the aerospace industry are involved—to cite only these few examples—every decision requires "cutting-edge" scientific and technical knowledge.

Since the elected official is not, except in rare cases, an expert in these scientific and technical fields, he or she is thus obliged to consult one or more experts.

But who are these experts whom I was chastising just a moment ago, who are being consulted by political leaders with an abysmal ignorance of the subject at hand? They are the high-level civil servants, who were around well before the elected officials took office, and therefore in a sense "inherited" them. Or they are associates appointed by the officials themselves. They may also be advisers taken on by the elected officials because they were recommended by mutual friends, by persons with whom the politicians want to curry favor, or lastly because they are relatives or personal friends. Finally they might be scientists, generally academics, who are not part of either the government or the political scene, but whom the officials, confronted with a problem, happen to consult.

The social, economic, and political importance of the questions being addressed is sometimes enormous: choosing a futuristic strategy which will thus be proportionately very expensive and highly sophisticated, no matter what its eventual effectiveness; choosing a policy to protect the environment and manage the chemistry of materials PCBs (polychlorinated biphenyls) a while ago or CFCs (chlorofluorocarbons) today—that will mean tens of millions of dollars wasted if the choice is bad, but saved if it is correct; choosing a technology for some major government-subsidized industry; choosing a policy for dams intended to control river flooding, within one's own borders or in the underdeveloped countries to which one claims to be providing assistance. Not to mention the innumerable choices, justified or not, which are made on the advice of scientists who are reasonably close to power but of lesser status, from sniffer aircraft to Science City, from forest fire management to the siting of steel mills.

Given the extraordinary expansion of scientific knowledge and the extreme narrowness of these almost innumerable disciplines, it has now become impossible for any researcher to possess the expertise needed to express a qualified opinion on a question outside his or her own specialty. Beyond its boundaries, no matter how encyclopedic the scientist's education, he or she cannot give a truly authoritative opinion today; the best counsel that the politician can expect from such advisers concerns their choice of some other expert or experts.

Returning to earthquake protection and more specifically to earthquake prediction, the politicians responsible for disaster prevention, because they neither have nor claim to have any expertise in the subject, rely on scientific personalities who are considered competent because of their hierarchical position or their profession.

It is unfortunate that when these persons are, for example, geochemists or seismologists, they do not possess that characteristic. It may seem paradoxical that a seismologist is not qualified in the matter of earthquake prediction, but it is nevertheless quite true: not only, after half a century of costly effort, has no seismologist managed to predict an earthquake, but moreover the advisers in question have never targeted their own research in that direction. Seismology is after all a basic science, which studies the interior of the Earth by recording, analyzing, and interpreting seismic waves. It is the discipline which, almost single-handedly, has allowed us to gain a general idea of our planet that is apparently close to reality. But all this fundamental seismology has never managed to predict a single earthquake.

The economic and human significance of destructive earthquakes has of course led several seismologists to look for ways of predicting them. We know, however, that these efforts have not produced any positive results and that the VAN method, the only effective one so far, is not based in any way on the use of seismographic records: it is based not on seismology but, as we shall see, on solid-state physics and the intelligent interpretation of a geophysical signal.

We may well wonder why certain governmental authorities have not felt the need to give their countries the benefits of the VAN method, although everyone should be able to recognize its amazing effectiveness. How many more years will have to pass before a network of stations, suitably calibrated in terms of the seismogenic zones surrounding them, is sufficiently operational to protect the population from the killer earthquakes which are almost certain to occur soon? Must we wait for the next disaster and then, as usual, do nothing afterwards?

This situation demonstrates the tremendous importance of establishing ethical rules to codify the selection of scientific experts who are called upon to advise political figures. The problem is what we might call the "Lysenko syndrome," after that Russian agronomist whose intellectual rigor was no match for his intelligence, and whose ambition became evident from his contempt for his colleagues' reputations. Lysenko had managed to gain Stalin's ear, and took advantage of his position to see that the best Soviet geneticists—who at that time were among the finest in the world—were stripped of their positions and sent to concentration camps. Today, forty years later, genetics in the USSR has still not recovered from that tragedy.

Fortunately there are no concentration camps today in the United States or in France, but the harm done both to science and to public safety by rampant "Lysenkoism" is no less serious. It would be well for public opinion to take note of this, and, through their elected officials and the institutions of a democracy, for citizens to make sure that the greater good of the nation is not sacrificed to the maneuvering of sycophants.

This applies to every country and every political system on Earth.

II

WHAT IS

AN EARTHQUAKE?

What is an earthquake? It can be defined as a movement, transient and temporary, caused by the sudden release of stresses that have accumulated for years, or tens or even hundreds of years, in the region where it occurs. The move ment generally takes place along a pre-existing fault, in other words a fissure affecting the rocks of the Earth's crust, which "moves" from time to time over hundreds of millennia. The closer to the surface and the more widely separated in time, the more formidable the earthquakes will be.

Elastic waves then propagate from the fractured zone, covering distances which vary depending on the nature and magnitude of the tremor, but can range between tens and thousands of kilometers. In an area of variable size around the propagation focus, these waves shake the ground sufficiently to destabilize and imperil the structures that humans have built upon it.

THE STRUCTURE OF THE PLANET

It is only because some readers might have forgotten that I insert this brief reminder: our planet can be compared to an egg—an egg about 12,700 km [7,900 mi] in diameter. In other words, the Earth approximately resembles a sphere with a thin outer shell, a "white," and a "yolk." The

thickness of the Earth's shell, which in geological jargon
we call the lithosphere (Greek *lithos* = stone), is not much
greater, proportionately, than that of an eggshell: from
barely a half-dozen kilometers [some three and a half
miles] (in Spring 1971 Léon Steinmetz measured this minimum thickness in the Gulf of Tadjoura near Djibouti) to
about 100 km [60 mi] under high mountain ranges. Compared to the radius of the Earth (6,380 km or 3,950 mi), this
shell is therefore truly very thin—and fragile. When it
cracks it emits waves, somewhat like a pebble tossed into a
pond. When these waves are large the ground vibrates, so
much so that sometimes it brings down what human beings
have erected, or even what Nature itself has built up.

Beneath this shell of hard rock lies the "white" of the
terrestrial egg, which is almost 2,900 km [1,800 mi] thick
and which Earth-science specialists call the mantle because
it surrounds the "yolk," which is called the liquid core. This
core in turn surrounds the inner, or solid, core which, at a
depth of about 5,000 km [3,000 mi], constitutes the central
sphere of the planet. The mantle itself is divided into the
upper mantle and lower mantle (or mesosphere); the upper
part of the upper mantle is a spherical layer that has been
dubbed the asthenosphere, to emphasize how weak it is
(Greek *astheneia* = weakness). This "weakness" probably
results from partial melting of the rocks.

The asthenosphere is therefore fluid, at least when the
forces applied to it do not exceed certain limits and continue
for sufficient lengths of time. In this respect it is like ice,
which acts like a solid when hit sharply with a hammer or

pick, but responds like a fluid to simple gravity when given enough time to do so: we know that glaciers flow down mountains under no pressure other than their own weight.

Revealed by studies of both seismic wave velocities and the subsidence (slow sinking of the Earth's crust under the weight of accumulated sediments) and uplift of crustal blocks, the fluidity of the asthenosphere is probably the source of most geological phenomena: movements of tectonic plates, folding of sediment layers that have piled up over the millions of years of geological epochs, uplifting of mountain ranges, volcanic eruptions... and earthquakes.

This model of our planet as a half-dozen nested concentric spheres—inner core, core, mesosphere, upper mantle, asthenosphere, and lithosphere—has essentially been constructed from the study of seismic waves, their propagation around the world, and the ways in which they are refracted and reflected at the discontinuities which separate these various spheres: without the science of seismology, we would not know much about the interior of the Earth.

The fundamental instrument of this discipline is the seismograph. This device is designed to record the elastic waves released at an earthquake's focus. Some of these waves have passed through the inner layers of the planet, while others have traversed the Earth's surface crust. The seismograph is based on the principle of inertia: a mass, which has been made as independent as possible of its support, remains relatively immobile when the support is suddenly jostled. The recording pointer, integral with the suspended mass, remains fixed while the recording paper (or the magnetic tape), integral with the frame and there-fore with the ground which is vibrating, records the various waves as they arrive.

Seismological interpretations of discontinuities, interpretations of changes in weight, calculations which indicate the density of the various concentric spheres, data provided by the study of eruptive rocks (that is, those that have come to the surface from the depths of the lithosphere or the asthenosphere), as well as the behavior of the various seismic waves in the successive layers that make up the planet—these are the components from which we have gained some idea of the nature, and certain properties, of these nested spheres.

The lithosphere, with an average density of 2.7, con-sists essentially of hard rock: granitic and sedimentary for the continents, and gabbroic and basaltic for the oceans. The asthenosphere, with a density on the order of 3.4, is made up of ultrabasic rocks (relatively poor in silica but rich in silicates and ferromagnesium oxides) that are partly molten and therefore fluid. The mantle probably has a sim-ilar petrographic and chemical composition, but its rocks are probably solid. The upper mantle may have a density between 3.5 and 4; the lower mantle (or mesosphere) between 4.5 and 6. The outer core, however, is likely to be completely different: it is liquid—since only shear waves, called S waves, can propagate through it—with a high den-sity (9.8–12), and it probably consists mainly of molten iron. The inner core, even denser (12–12.5), must be solid and made of metallic nickel.

PLATE TECTONICS

By 1910, Alfred Wegener had formulated his hypothesis stating that the continents moved with respect to one another and did not occupy today the successive positions that they had occupied in the geological past, nor those they would occupy in the future. Despite evidence from paleontology, stratigraphy, petrography, and geomorphology, almost every geologist and geophysicist refused, for half a century, to acknowledge this fact. One of the reasons was that Wegener was talking about continental "drift," which he compared to the movement of icebergs over the surface of the ocean. Well, since the ocean floors consisted of solid rock, the continents obviously cannot drift on them, any more than icebergs can drift through pack ice in winter. But another reason, an unstated one, was that Wegener was not a geologist but a meteorologist.

They were right to refute Wegener's hypothesis as far as the mechanisms of drift were concerned, but they were wrong to reject the drift itself. It took the discovery, in the late 1950s, of the phenomenon of sea-floor spreading to turn Wegener's detractors, suddenly, into his flatterers. Today almost everyone admits, not that the continents drift, but that they are carried along as the ocean floor spreads, each incorporated in a tectonic plate which is always partly oceanic. This spreading was demonstrated (predicted, observed, and measured *in situ*) in 1978 in the southern Afar region of Ethiopia, by my colleagues and me.

A new hypothesis can sometimes be rejected actively, by condemnation or derision, as was the case with Wegener; but sometimes—less aggressively but just as negatively—by silence and by "forgetting" it: one is unaware, or pretends to be unaware, of the uncomfortable theory; it is not referred to in meetings or mentioned in the bibliography of publications on the subject; everyone secretly hopes that this repeated forgetfulness will mean final oblivion for an idea that shocks the conformists and the careerists. This was, for example, what happened to the Milanković theory concerning the influence on glacial periods of astronomical factors such as changes in the relationship between the ecliptic and the Earth's axis of rotation, and in the ecliptic itself. As with Wegener's hypothesis, it took fifty years for this theory to be rescued from the oblivion to which it had deliberately been consigned. The astonishing coincidence is that Milanković was Wegener's son-in-law. Both of them had shocked the mandarins of their age, both suffered grievously for doing so, and both were already dead when their ideas were finally and universally acknowledged to be correct.

All too often, then, a revolutionary idea stimulates rejection rather than enthusiasm in the scientific world. The first impetus behind such rejection is intellectual prudence, which is admirable; but another reason is conformism, which is not. Lastly, it can be a sign of resentment, of envy at not having thought of the idea oneself; and that is not admirable at all.

Sea-floor spreading is based on those endless sequences of expansion fractures of the Earth's crust called "rifts," which succeed and connect to one another over a distance of more than 80,000 km [50,000 mi] around the entire globe. On either side of these rifts the ocean floors are moving apart: the age of their component rocks proves it, since they get older with distance. Thus the bottom of the Atlantic is "modern" along the axis of the rift, while it is 200 million years old near the coasts of Europe and Africa on one side, and the Americas on the other. The same is true for the much younger rift whose existence we discovered in Ethiopia: the Afar rift, an avatar of a future Erythrean Ocean consisting of the Red Sea, the Afar depression, and the Gulf of Aden. We found that the oceanic rocks constituting its floor were approximately 25 million years old at the edge of the great African continent to the west and the smaller Arabian continent to the east, but "zero age" along the axis of the rift itself, with the age increasing on either side of it.

Now confirmed by these observations and measurements, sea floor spreading is no longer simply a hypothesis but an established fact: the tectonic plate hypothesis can therefore in turn be regarded as a fact. The Earth's crust, in other words the lithosphere, must be described not as an intact eggshell but as a puzzle consisting of at least two dozen pieces fitted together abutting one another. These pieces of terrestrial "shell" are called tectonic or lithospheric plates. Some of them are immense, like the Eurasian plate which stretches from Japan to the Mid-Atlantic rift, or the African plate extending from the Mid-Atlantic rift to the Carlsberg rift in the Indian Ocean; others are more modest, like the Arabian plate, the Nazca plate, the Caribbean plate, or the micro-plates of the Mediterranean.

These plates always move away from generating rifts on the ocean floors; these rifts are also intercon-nected, forming one single fracture zone which extends around the globe for more than one and a half times its cir-cumference. This rift is also called a "ridge," since the mountains of lava (including the Hawaiian islands) built by the innumerable volcanoes along its length rise between 1,000 and 10,000 meters [3,300–33,000 ft] above the ocean floor. The Mid-Atlantic rift continues from west to east in the Southern Ocean around the Cape of Good Hope, halfway between Africa and Antarctica; then turns north again in the Indian Ocean halfway between Africa and Australia, then splits: one section runs northeast to form the Erythrean rift, while the other runs southeast, skirts Australia, and passes between it and Ant-arctica. Finally it crosses the southern part of the Pacific heading northeast, and enters the American continent through the Gulf of California.

The tectonic plates thus move away from each other on either side of this world-girdling rift: not only do the currents which agitate the hyperviscous fluids constitut-ing the asthenosphere drag along pieces of the thin lithospheric shell, but also the multitude of volcanoes which push apart the edges of the rift spew out millions and millions of cubic kilometers of lava. This lava, which solidifies almost instantly as soon as it emerges from the Earth, creates new sea floor. In fact it is not lava, but these "dikes"—walls of solidified magma in the fissures which once fed the eruptions—which are the fundamental constituents of the ocean floor.

If the volume of the planet were not constant, this expansion of the oceans would cause the Earth to "inflate." Such is not the case. Therefore the expansion of the ocean floors caused by the emergence of magma from the upper mantle must be compensated for, at other locations, by the disappearance into the depths of corresponding volumes of lithosphere. This is precisely what happens: a tectonic plate which is moving away from the rift—and is thus being pushed at its "stern"— bumps its "prow" into another tectonic plate. A collision then occurs. Since the laws of gravity and mechanics forbid these opposing tectonic plates to tilt up vertically in response to this collision, one of the two must pass under the other. But this phenomenon, called subduction (pulling under), varies depending on whether the impacting plates are oceanic or continental. The reason is simply that their densities are different: 2.7 on average for the continents, and approximately 3 for the oceans. So when a piece of ocean floor hits a continental plate, it dives under the continent: this is what is happening with the western Pacific and the Far East, and with the eastern Pacific and South America. And the plates dive at a steep angle, between 15° and 60°.

The term *Benioff plane* refers to the thin area, detected and pinpointed by seismologists, which is the location of the foci of the tremors that accompany the plate as it descends. These earthquakes are shallow in places where the plate begins its dive at a long, narrow, and deep oceanic trench, for example east of Japan, south of the Aleutians, east of the Philippines, or south of Indonesia. As the plate penetrates deeper, the focus depth increases. The greatest depth at which an earthquake has been recorded is 700 km [over 400 mi], in other words, within the asthenosphere itself.

The same process occurs when two oceanic plates meet: the denser of the two sinks into the upper mantle. When two continental plates collide, however, the one which passes underneath is too light (density 2.7) to penetrate into the asthenosphere, whose density is 3.4: it therefore slips between the asthenosphere and the continental plate which "floats" above it, raising the latter to extraordinary altitudes: this is the mechanism which is elevating the Himalayas, Tibet, Tianshan—the Roof of the World.

Lesser mountains such as the Alps, the Andes, or the ranges of Japan are also produced by subduction, but this time because an oceanic plate has moved beneath a continental plate. The sediments resulting from erosion of the above-water part of the continent, which have accumulated on its underwater extension called the "continental shelf," gradually tilt as subduction starts to form the marginal trench; the sediments then fold and are converted into hard rocks, which, under stress, crack, split, and fault. The movement of each fault causes an earthquake of a particular energy, which releases some of the accumulated stress.

As these enormous thicknesses of sediment are folded and compressed, their density—which was about 1.5–2 originally and reaches 2.7 when they have finally turned to rock and metamorphosed, but is still light compared to deeper rocks—increases. Since all this happens in the long, narrow marginal trench, the mountain range which results is also long and narrow.

OBSTACLES TO EARTHQUAKES

The Earth's seismicity is almost entirely a result of this enormous plate tectonic activity, whether the shocks accompany rift spreading, subduction, or the movement between two plates which, instead of colliding, "slide" against one another—like the North American and Pacific plates or, on a slightly more modest scale, sections of a single plate which slide along one another in successive releases of stress.

These movements, which are probably driven by magma currents in the upper mantle, are nevertheless not as continuous and regular as the currents themselves undoubtedly are, since the Earth's crust is so heterogeneous that it presents numerous obstacles: these obstacles block the movements of the lithospheric plates and immobilize them at certain locations from time to time.

Imagine that you have to push a safe that weighs 500 pounds, not along a smooth floor but along a dirt road. Your progress will be halted by every rough spot a quarter-inch or so high, and you will then need to push harder to overcome that little obstacle, which will then suddenly give way. If the relief is on the order of a few inches, you will be stuck until the force that you have to build up exceeds the mechanical strength threshold of the obstacle; at that point the obstacle will suddenly break and your safe can proceed to the next rough spot. Staying with this same model but replacing the safe with a block of the Earth's crust sliding by friction along another block, an earthquake will correspond to the sudden relaxation of the stresses that have gradually accumulated at depth in front of each obstacle, and that relaxation will be expressed by a sudden movement—with differential sliding on either side of the fault—of the two crustal blocks in question.

This elastic rebound creates mechanical waves, which propagate within the Earth at speeds ranging from about 2 km/s to about 14 km/s, depending on the type of wave, the nature of the terrain, and the depth. Two types of elastic wave are produced when this process begins: volume waves and surface waves. Volume waves are either P waves or S waves. P waves are faster, and arrive at the seismographic station first; S waves are slower and arrive later. The "P" stands for pressure waves, which vibrate along the direction of propagation, while the "S" indicates shear waves, which vibrate in a plane perpendicular to their propagation.

Surface waves are either Love waves, which vibrate horizontally and transverse to the propagation radius; or Rayleigh waves, which propagate rather like swells on the sea. The surface waves generated by a particular earthquake are generally of much greater amplitude than the volume waves, and are therefore much more dangerous. The S waves are also more formidable when the earthquake is of sufficient magnitude and its focus is less than a thousand kilometers away.

P waves can pass through both liquids and solids, while S waves are stopped by liquids and are slowed down by a partly fluid medium like the asthenosphere. These properties enabled seismologists to demonstrate that the asthenosphere is partly molten, that the mantle and inner core are solid, and that the core is fluid.

When a tremor is sufficiently strong the P and S waves pass through the entire planet (although the S waves are stopped and reflected by the liquid outer core), and the surface waves (Love and Rayleigh waves), which are slower than the P and S waves, have much greater amplitudes with longer periods.

The displacement of the crustal material (its vibration) is proportional to the "seismic moment" which characterizes the magnitude of the source. It is inversely proportional, however, to the distance traveled and to the cube of the velocity. The seismic moment is sometimes regarded as the factor that best represents the size of an earthquake. It is equal to the surface area of the fault plane being displaced, multiplied by the average displacement distance and the modulus of rigidity of the rocks involved.

The significance of an earthquake shock for human beings depends on a number of factors, but principally on the location of its epicenter: in a highly populated or in a deserted area, under a city or in the countryside, in flat terrain or on the side of a mountain, etc. Leaving this aside, we must also consider the strictly seismic characteristics: depth of focus, amount of energy released—which can be expressed either by the magnitude (calculated) or by the seismic moment (also calculated from signals recorded by seismograph networks)—but also accelerations of the ground at a particular location, vibration amplitude and frequency, the duration of the shock (which can range from a few seconds to a few minutes), and much more.

Acceleration and duration are the essential factors which explain the destruction of buildings and the break-down of certain fragile natural equilibria: it is believed that such breakdowns can lead to landslides and, in moun-tainous areas, to avalanches and to the release of enormous torrents caused by the melting of glaciers.

MAGNITUDE AND INTENSITY

I have deliberately omitted any discussion of deep-seated earthquakes (more than 150 km), since even the strongest of them rarely have any destructive effects, and their mechanisms are different. We have seen that destructive earthquakes are produced by a sudden shift in a portion of the Earth's crust along a fault or a series of parallel faults. The greater the shift—in terms of both the mass involved and the distance traveled by that mass—the longer the earthquake will be and the greater the energy released; that energy is expressed in degrees of magnitude. The higher the magnitude, the more violent and numerous the shocks (called "aftershocks") which will continue to occur, sometimes for almost a year or more, after the prin-cipal shock—and (assuming a constant distance from the focus) the more intense its effects, in other words the *intensity* of the earthquake.

Of every 1,000 earthquakes, 999 occur in long, narrow zones that are now well defined: these are the "earthquake belts" that snake their way around the globe. It has been known since the late 1950s that these belts correspond to the edges of tectonic plates (see map on pp. 20–21). That remaining one-in-a-thousand earthquake must not be underestimated, however; far from it. Earthquakes which occur outside the continuously affected areas, although very rare, are sometimes terribly violent. Moreover, they are unexpected: several centuries may pass between two "intraplate" earthquakes, while "interplate" seismicity is continuous and therefore much less surprising. The best known of these intraplate earthquakes was the one at New Madrid, Missouri in 1811.

According to Charles Richter, the originator of the idea of seismic magnitude, the earthquake that reached the highest-ever estimated magnitude did not occur in any of the known seismic areas, but in Portugal, a country almost as seismically placid as France or Switzerland: this was the Lisbon earthquake of 1755, which had such exceptional effects—it even caused standing waves to appear in the lakes of Finland and northern Russia—that its energy must have corresponded to a 9 on the Richter scale! Its true magnitude can never be known, because that value must be *calculated*, using an empirical formula, from the amplitude of a certain type of seismic wave recorded by a seismograph. Since that instrument was not invented until the end of the 19th century (by John Milne), we have no seismograms of the 1755 Lisbon earthquake, and its magnitude therefore can only be estimated. This was done, on the basis of a family of recent tremors in this region, by determining the ratio between magnitude and maximum intensity. That ratio was then simply applied to the 1755 earthquake, whose intensity is known from published descriptions.

Magnitudes are distributed *continuously* on the Richter scale, which does not range from 0 to 9 as too many people think (and, what is worse, write), but from minus infinity to plus infinity: it is what mathematicians call an open-ended scale. Richter had assigned a magnitude of 0 to the mildest Earth tremor that could be detected at that time (the late 1930s) by what was called a Wood-Anderson seismograph. But with technological progress it is now possible to record earthquakes that are 10 to 20 times weaker, and they therefore have negative magnitudes. The maximum magnitude, around 9, is limited by the mechanical properties of rocks: when the stresses acting on them reach their rupture strength threshold, they break and move, triggering the shock.

The effects (or intensities) of an earthquake are expressed on a *discontinuous* scale from I to XII, each graduation of which corresponds to about twice the destruction of the previous one. Every earthquake has many intensities, depending on where they are measured, which decrease from the strongest, generally located at the epicenter (the point on the Earth's surface directly above the focus—the *hypocenter*, in seismological jargon), to areas where the earthquake was not felt and where its intensity is therefore zero. However an earthquake can only have one single magnitude, just as a bomb is characterized by its weight of explosive (magnitude) whose effects (intensity) decrease with distance.

It is worth emphasizing that what counts, in terms of the risks involved, is not the magnitude but the intensity. It is after all the intensity which determines whether an earthquake is or is not destructive, does or does not kill. There have been many earthquakes with high magnitudes but acceptable intensities, either because the focus was deep-seated or because the region was sparsely populated. On the other hand, there have been numerous earthquakes with magnitudes less than 6 that have been of catastrophic intensity: IX or even X MSK (MSK are the initials of the seismologists—Medvedev, Shebalin, and Karnik—who defined the gradations). The intensity scale gives an idea of the effects of a tremor. Intensity depends on magnitude, of course, but also on distance from the epicenter, depth of focus, and the response of the soil to the many different stresses caused by seismic waves.

There are three types of stresses which bring rocks to their breaking point: tension, compression, and shear. Tensile stresses rarely cause earthquakes with magnitudes greater than 6 on the Richter scale. The others, compression and shear, are what unleash most of the seismic catastrophes.

This is why major earthquakes occur mostly in areas where the Earth's crust is being compressed, in other words where two tectonic plates are colliding with or sliding against one another. When they collide, the denser one inevitably passes under the other one, which then "rides" over it. This explains why China is the most earthquake-plagued nation on Earth—unlike any other country, it has the unfortunate distinction of riding on two tectonic plates at once: the oceanic West Pacific plate, and the continental Indian plate.

Oceanic plates, as we have seen, are relatively heavy because they consist exclusively of gabbroic and basaltic rocks, with an average density of 2.8–3. Thus when they meet a lighter continental plate, they necessarily pass beneath it. Continental plates are less dense because they consist essentially of granite and of sedimentary rocks. The oceanic Pacific plate arrives from the east and dives under Japan and eastern China, that is, under the continental Asian plate, at an angle that can be very accurately determined from calculations of seismic focus depths, and ranges between 15° and 75°. Arriving from the south, the Indian plate also passes beneath the Asian plate because the front part of the former—which was an ocean floor that has now been engulfed in the asthenosphere by subduction—has already been dragged under Asia. The continental portion, which is less dense, must—and I am deliberately repeating this—force its way almost horizontally underneath the Asian plate, causing the gargantuan uplift dubbed the "Roof of the World": the Himalayas, Karakorum, Kunlun, the Hindu Kush, the Pamirs, the Tianshan plateau, the high plateau of Tibet, etc. This entire process results in tremendous earthquakes, more numerous than anywhere else; but fortunately they occur in relatively sparsely populated areas.

No comparable situation exists anywhere else, at least not in our present geological epoch: a single continental plate riding over two tectonic plates, one of which is also continental. The latter case is in itself exceptional, and only a single other instance is known: as the Arabian plate moves northeastwards, it passes beneath Iran and gives rise to the Zagros mountains and the high plateaus which follow them, and to the strong seismic activity of the region.

Everywhere else, at present, every plate undergoing subduction is oceanic. These plates dive into the mantle at a steep angle, either when they collide with a continental plate—for example the confrontations between the eastern Pacific plate and the Americas, the western Pacific and the Far East, and the Indian Ocean and Southeast Asia (Indonesia and Indochina)—or when two oceanic plates meet one another, like the Pacific plates that are colliding near Vanuatu and Fiji, or the northern Pacific plate that is being subducted under the Arctic, or the western Atlantic plates, one of which is penetrating under the Caribbean and the other under the southern Antilles.

The steep angle at which subduction occurs in each of these cases explains why the width of mountain uplift caused by the encounter is relatively modest—60 to 120 miles—or even zero. Conversely, the Roof of the World is more than 600 miles wide because it results from subhorizontal subduction of a continental plate. The present-day distribution of earthquakes is closely linked to the genesis of geologically young mountains.

III

PREDICTING

EARTHQUAKES

The seismic history of a country begins, at the earliest, with the local invention of writing or at least with our ability to decipher it. That is why the great American civilizations—Aztec, Maya, Inca—have so far been able to tell us nothing about the subject, although they managed to construct buildings that would resist the terrible Andean Earth tremors: Machu Picchu is still an outstanding example of earthquake-resistant architecture. The Chinese, the only culture to have enjoyed a 3,000-year history of literate civilization, thus have the world's longest seismic history, which moreover concerns the most earthquake-ridden country on Earth, in which human beings have been trying to predict earthquakes for at least four millennia.

As far as France is concerned, its seismic history does not begin until 1356, with the enormous earthquake at Basel (actually in Switzerland). This tremor, the oldest yet found in our written records, reached an intensity of XI MSK: everything was destroyed, including castles, within a radius of thirty miles or so, and well-constructed buildings (such as monasteries and churches) were demolished as far away as 250 miles from the epicenter, particularly at Avallon.

The second known "French" earthquake was the one at Prats de Mollo in Catalonia in 1428. The chronicles of the day recorded its misdeeds: the destruction inflicted on castles, churches, and monasteries—the only buildings worth mentioning at that time—extended up to 250 miles from the epicenter, to Barcelona, Le Puy, and Leghorn. Its intensity was therefore also XI MSK.

The third large-scale French earthquake occurred in 1564 just north of Nice. On the basis of available descriptions it has been assigned an intensity of X MSK, which corresponds to effects half as severe as those of a XI tremor, but twice as great as those of a IX quake. For comparison, IX MSK was the intensity of the earthquakes at Orléansville in 1954, Agadir in 1960, El Asnam in 1980, Mexico in 1985, and Armenia in 1989; and about twenty tremors of this intensity have been recorded in France during the last 600 years.

We have seen that an earthquake is a geological phenomenon governed by the relative motions of tectonic plates. We also know that a particular geological phenomenon will continue in a given region for tens of millions of years. Its presence in that region is thus, on a human scale, "eternal." We can therefore state that if a major earthquake has occurred at a particular place on even a single historically recorded occasion, other tremors at least as powerful will occur there in the future. And—a self-evident truth that we must not forget—the farther back in time the last seismic catastrophe, the more imminent the next one.

We can also state that the longer a period of seismic calm continues, the ruder the awakening is likely to be.

This is in fact the probable reason for the magnitude of 9 on the Richter scale reached by the Lisbon earthquake, since it took place in a region that is only rarely affected. This was also why the three New Madrid tremors of 1811 had such high magnitudes (8 or even more), and were felt almost 1,200 miles from the epicenter.

The reason is that a seismic lull, characterized by the absence not only of high-energy shocks but also of the more usual moderate tremors, definitely does not mean any interruption in the ultimate causes of seismic activity. As we have seen, the causes that produce movements of tectonic plates are probably currents agitating the fluid portions of the planet's upper mantle, which drive the lithospheric plates whose bases are immersed in the asthenosphere. And it is extremely probable that, like ocean currents, these currents never stop or even experience significant changes, except on a scale of millions of years.

So when earthquake activity in a region ceases for five or ten years, or even for a few centuries, it is not because the magma currents, the prime movers of seismic activity, have stopped or slowed down, but probably for some mechanical reason: because the rocks are resisting for a longer period than usual the stresses that are being placed on them. As long as they continue to resist, the mechanical stresses induced by the underlying magma current will continue to accumulate, just as they do in an iron bar that is being squeezed harder and harder in a vise. And the crustal rocks, like the iron bar, will take longer to break and will break more violently, the longer their greater strength has allowed them to resist.

Note carefully now: it has been eighty years since France has experienced an intensity IX tremor, and 500 years since an intensity X or XI quake; and the eastern United States has not had a major earthquake for almost two centuries!

SOLID SKEPTICISM

Before 1984 I believed it was impossible to predict earthquakes, and I thought it would always be so. I repeated that assertion at every opportunity, and the extraordinary success of the Chinese—who in 1975 announced the great Haicheng (Liaoning) earthquake in time to evacuate the population—was only, I said, the exception that proved the rule. It was the one single success in more than a quarter-century of costly effort undertaken by all the major nations threatened by destructive earthquakes—essentially the United States, Soviet Union, China, and Japan—a single success out of hundreds of killer quakes that were not predicted: that's a pretty exceptional exception!

The reasons for my skepticism appeared solid, ranging from the impossibility of conducting on-site research deep inside the Earth where earthquakes are caused to the complexity of the natural phenomena involved. A comparison with the difficulties faced by meteorologists trying to forecast the weather merely confirmed my belief. Not only can weather forecasters contemplate a transparent and easily accessible atmosphere—rather than the impenetrable, opaque planet that confronts seismologists—but the resources available to them are also incomparably more impressive than those of the geophysicists: from super-computers to artificial satellites, from weather balloons to meteorological helicopters and airplanes, not to mention thousands of observation points and hundreds of thousands of specialized personnel. The importance of weather prediction for aerial and maritime navigation, for agriculture, for the tourist industry and above all for all the world's armed forces, explains the size of meteorology budgets. Earthquakes, on the other hand, mean nothing to any of these rich and powerful pressure groups. Moreover, the fact that no one had ever managed to predict a destructive earthquake, aside from that single success in 1975, reinforced me in my refusal to be hopeful about this subject which I considered hopeless.

The subject of this line of inquiry was important, however, to the earthquake prevention specialist that I had gradually become since the on-site study that I had made, in May and June of 1960, of the colossal earthquake in southern Chile, whose magnitude of 8.7 remains the highest recorded this century. I therefore kept up to date with investigations in progress, and could not help but notice that the hopes raised here and there by some new approach were always dashed. For example, consider the approach which says that the longer the period of seismic inactivity following a great earthquake in a given region, the greater the risk that the tremor which ends that lull will be violent and imminent. This hypothesis, which is rational and also widely supported by the facts, has so far unfortunately provided none of the essential information—location, intensity, date—that would make it possible to alert threatened populations in time, and to take the necessary preventive actions.

Not only does this approach not localize, within 50 or even 150 miles, the epicenter of the future tremor, or give any estimate of its magnitude or the depth of its focus—two parameters with which its intensity could be predicted—but it does not give even the vaguest idea of approximately when the dreaded shock will occur (a few years from now? a few decades?). As an example, for more than a dozen years seismologists have been warning of the imminent occurrence of a major earthquake in the Kanto region, which stretches from Tokyo to the Izu peninsula, an area that was badly shaken in 1923 with the loss of almost 200,000 lives. But knowing that a large-scale quake will occur again, without being able to say if it will happen today, next year, or twenty years from now, nor being able to specify within 50 miles *where* it will happen, is not much help to those responsible for the population's survival, nor to the people themselves.

Another example is the earthquake that claimed tens of thousands of victims in Mexico in 1985: it had been anticipated (and even predicted) by seismologists for years, since a particularly calm and prolonged gap characterized the Pacific coast in the area near Colima, where it finally did occur. But they were unable to determine, even to the nearest decade, when it might happen. Or where. Or with what intensity. Hence the appalling loss of life. Once again, when the December 7, 1988, earthquake struck in Armenia, it had been more than half a century since that region had been hit by a major tremor: of course the specialists were aware of the "seismic gap," but their knowledge stopped right there. A few years ago, using the same seismic gap hypothesis, an American expert made his own analysis of the gap and predicted a destructive earthquake in Peru. The result was panic, evacuation of the capital city of Lima, a shutdown in economic activity… but nothing happened. Imagine the cost of such mistakes!

Thus any seismologist or geologist with any competence at all, knowing the gaps that exist in the various seismic zones, can predict without fear of error that a major earthquake will occur there, today or in half a dozen centuries: near Lisbon or Basel, around Friuli or Nice, in California, Missouri, or Japan. But the practical utility of such a prediction is not evident.

As far as the method which relies on precursor tremors is concerned, it too has almost never successfully predicted an important quake, first of all because destructive earthquakes are only very rarely preceded by precursor shocks, and also, perhaps primarily, because so far we have no way of differentiating between these precursor shocks and the moderate-magnitude earthquakes which are ordinary events in any seismic region.

Three other classic approaches have been used in an attempt to predict earthquakes: one is as old as Chinese civilization, the second as young as this century, and the last made its debut in 1960 on the occasion of the 8.7 magnitude quake in Chile. The first is based on the interpretation of certain foreshadowing signs, such as animal behavior, the flow of springs, the level of groundwater in wells, etc. The second approach is based on the observation, reported for the first time in 1898 by John Milne—one of the great names in the history of seismology and, as we have noted, inventor of the seismograph—that the telluric current record exhibited an unmistakable signal prior to the great tremor in Assam in 1897. The third, no doubt very closely related to the second, consists in attempting to interpret the preseismic significance of the electromagnetic signal—transmitted through the atmosphere like any radio signal—that was observed for the first time by an American astrophysicist in California, six days before the terrible seismic shocks of May 20 and 21, 1960 in Chile.

The Chinese have been trying to predict earthquakes for some 4,000 years. Long before the modern era and the sophisticated instruments with which science has now endowed us, the Chinese had invented other devices, including a "seismoscope" that indicated the relative intensity and direction of the tremors. Consequently they had also accumulated innumerable observations concerning phenomena which sometimes appeared to precede major earthquakes: obvious restlessness in certain animals, sometimes all of them, expressed either as unusual silence (especially of birds) or as vocalizations such as neighing, barking, bleating, cackling, howling, or squealing; or as unusual movements of reptiles, agitated behavior by fish, birds, and mammals, etc.

In addition, it was at least partly by interpreting these animal reactions and by observing changes in the flow of springs or in groundwater levels, but also on the basis of an impressive body of precise geophysical measurements—magnetic field variations, microseismic activity, radon gas emissions, changes in electrical resistivity, ground elevation, or the distance between two or more points on the surface, increased tremor frequency, changes in seismic wave propagation velocity and the ratio between P wave velocity and S wave velocity (which appears to be a very promising parameter)—that Chinese seismologists succeeded in making their admirable prediction of the 1975 Liaoning earthquake. Sounding the alarm on the very morning of the catastrophe, they saved hundreds of thousands of people from death or permanent injury.

Unfortunately the precursor signs perceived by animals do not appear before every major quake, and their interpretation is far from completely understood, even in China. Animals' perception capabilities might, quite logically, decrease rapidly with the depth of the seismic focus. Similarly, it is only on very exceptional occasions that geophysical parameters—which on this occasion had corroborated the predictions based on observations of Nature—yield information that can be interpreted in terms of prediction. And the same seismologists who had succeeded so magnificently in 1975 were unable to predict the disaster that occurred the next year in the same region, destroying the city of Tangshan, killing almost a million people, and injuring a number that has never been revealed.

Reported for the first time in 1898 by John Milne before the Royal Society in London, the observation that, before every sufficiently powerful earthquake, a signal seems to affect the telluric currents—the natural Earth currents which circulate throughout the ground—has since been repeatedly confirmed. And many seismologists, thereafter and in many different countries (India, Russia, China, the United States, Japan) tried to detect this precursor signal and use it to predict the place and date of the earthquake that it was theoretically foreshadowing. The effort was unfortunately in vain, and this approach to the problem was almost completely abandoned.

THE VAN METHOD

For many years, therefore, I had stopped believing that it was possible to predict earthquakes. Then, on the occasion of an official visit that I was making to Athens in the context of a cooperative French-Greek project that I had initiated—designed to improve the effectiveness of the relief efforts needed after any large-scale disaster by combining the resources of our two countries—I was interviewed by Greek television about the purpose of my visit. I explained the problem of organizing relief work, which today is quite scandalously inadequate all over the world, and mentioned the reforms that I had been trying for two years to have implemented in France.

I was then asked what I thought of earthquake prediction as a preventive measure. I set forth the reasons for my skepticism. The journalist then replied: "What about the VAN method?" "What's the VAN method?" I asked. He explained it to me briefly, and my response was that I doubted whether these three Greek scientists Varotsos, Alexopoulos, and Nomikos, whose initials were the acronym designating the method, could have succeeded where the world's most famous seismologists, with all the dollars, rubles, yen, and yuan of their respective rich nations behind them, had completely failed.

A few days later after I had returned to Paris, I received a letter from Professor Alexopoulos (the "A" in VAN). He said he had been informed that I was not familiar with their method (which was absolutely true), and asked if I would please read the two articles that he had enclosed with the letter. I groaned silently: my unhappy experience with volcanology treatises, sent to me occasionally by far too many inventors, amateurs, and so-called specialists, made me wonder whether these articles would be in a similar vein. But as soon as I took them out of the envelope I began to take them more seriously: they had been published in *Tectonophysics*, a prestigious international journal.

As every scientist already knows, an article that discusses science can almost never make it into print in a leading journal without penetrating those formidable barriers called "referees." These reviewers are, theoretically, specialists in the subject of the article in question, and are therefore (again theoretically) competent to render an opinion, favorable or otherwise, as to whether it should be published. Theoretically again, they are honest and their judgment is not affected either by their personal reactions to the author or the hypothesis advocated by the article, or by the effects which it might have on their own work, their personal reputation, or their own credibility. Of course it does happen that some reviewers do not always adhere to the ethic that is presumed to govern them, but I am still convinced, despite all the disillusionment accumulated over fifty years of experience, that most of them do respect it.

The fact that "Physical Properties of the Variations of the Electric Field of the Earth Preceding Earthquakes" appeared in *Tectonophysics* constituted, once the usual potential reservations had been set aside, a strong presumption that the work was serious and of high quality. That fact ensured that the authors of the article were probably neither dreamers nor charlatans.

I therefore began reading with interest, and when I had finished I was rather taken aback: my conviction that it was impossible to predict earthquakes had just been undermined.

The VAN method consists in continuously recording telluric currents using a network of stations which cover a particular region. These ubiquitous natural electrical currents are induced by the continual changes experienced by the Earth's magnetic field, whatever the location or the cause. They are concentrated very close to the surface, and the ease with which they circulate depends on the resistivity of the soil; they move more often in sheets of electricity than in narrow channels. Émile Thellier, professor of geophysics and one of the founding fathers of French geomagnetism research, has said than in flat terrain, the magnetic field is parallel to the surface, and that it can be completely characterized by measuring it along two telluric lines placed at right angles.

This is what Varotsos and his two collaborators decided to do for the region of continental Greece by setting up sixteen stations around the country, each of them comprising an arrangement of two perpendicular sensors. The Greek islands, in both the Aegean and Ionian Seas, do not yet have any stations, but that is simply for lack of financial resources.

Each of these stations consists of at least two sensors, one oriented north-south and the other east-west. The principle of these sensors is very simple: two electrodes buried in the ground several dozen, hundred, or even thousand feet apart, connected by a conductive wire to a voltage amplifier and a chart recorder. This system can then continuously record the low-voltage currents which circulate in the ground, and can detect Milne's famous signal, the SES (seismic electrical signal) that always seems to precede an earthquake.

The intensity of this signal is proportional to the energy of the earthquake that it foreshadows, and inversely proportional to its distance from the station. Small shocks—less than magnitude 3 on the Richter scale—create signals that are correspondingly small and therefore difficult to distinguish from background noise. Major quakes, however, produce a well-defined SES.

This seismic electrical signal most often occurs as a sudden deviation, positive or negative, in the monotonous line plotted by the telluric current. This deviation, representing a few millivolts, rapidly reaches its maximum amplitude, and for a few minutes or a few dozen minutes the trace then continues parallel to the initial line. The deviation disappears just as suddenly as it started, and the signal therefore usually draws a rectangle or trapezoid along the abscissa, whose length depends on the duration. This duration and the amplitude (measured along the ordinate) are the parameters from which, using empirical formulas worked out by the three physicists Varotsos, Alexopoulos, and Nomikos, the magnitude and distance of the coming earthquake can then be calculated.

The amplitude of the signal obviously depends both on the magnitude of the shock that it is announcing and on the distance between the future epicenter and the receiving station. If at least three stations have recorded the signal, the epicenter can be easily and accurately located. If only two have recorded it a certain uncertainty remains, and if only one, then the uncertainty is certain. Except…

The exception, as the experience of the last few years has taught us, is that if the precursor signal of at least one prior earthquake has been recorded by the station, that station is thereafter calibrated with respect to the region where that earthquake took place subsequent to the SES. In other words, the SES that is picked up at a given station from a given seismic region has characteristics that are recognizable from then on.

On February 1, 1988, Bernard Massinon, his colleague Alain Leroy and I had the good fortune, on arriving in Athens where we would be meeting with Varotsos, to find that an SES had just been recorded after weeks of inactivity. Two stations had received it, one at Salonika in the northern part of the country and the other in Athens. And Varotsos had waited, allowing us to participate in the interpretation of these signals: an extraordinarily rare example of generosity amid the all too common egocentricity of the academic and scientific research world.

We spent half a dozen hours in discussions, particularly about the ambiguity resulting from the fact that, when plotted with the receiving stations at the center and the distance calculated from the signal amplitude as the radius, the two circumferences intersected at two different points. The ambiguity was resolved by means of SESs and their corresponding tremors that had recently been recorded at one, the other, or both of the stations: the polarity of the signals (positive or negative), their amplitudes, their ratios, and the north-south and east-west components of their traces finally allowed us to eliminate the east coast of Thessaly—the earthquakes that had occurred there previously had yielded precursor signals with characteristics different from those of the SESs on that day of February 1, 1988. At about 1:00 in the morning on February 2, Professor Varotsos sent a confidential telegram to the Permanent Interministerial Committee responsible for preventive measures, announcing that a magnitude 5 ($\pm$ 0.5) earthquake was imminent, and stating that its epicenter would be located 200 km [125 mi] northeast of Athens, namely in the Aegean Sea near the southwest coast of the island of Lesbos.

Ten days later, on February 11, the shock occurred just where the calculations had placed it, and with a magnitude of 4.7 on the Richter scale. The last four of those very long days of waiting seemed interminable to me, since, during the seven years of experience that I had accumulated in this field, the longest time span between detection of a signal and the actual earthquake that it indicated had been seven days.

If only a single station has received the signal, it is still possible to predict the epicenter and the magnitude of the quake, but only if the station and the seismic zone have been mutually calibrated by means of at least one prior SES. The characteristics of the seismic zone will then have been determined, along with the "response" of the station in question. This was why, on September 1, 1988, Varotsos was able to predict the magnitudes and epicenter locations, which he sent by telegraph to the *ad hoc* interministerial committee, of four tremors which were indicated to him by four SESs received only by the station at Ioannina; the magnitude predicted for the most violent of them was between 5.3 and 5.8. These earthquakes took place on September 5, 6, 11, and 22, with magnitudes of 4.0, 4.2, 4.3, and 5.5. The last one was fairly destructive.

On September 29 and 30, the same station at Ioannina—and once again that one alone—received eight SESs from the same region approximately 240 km [150 mi] west of Athens. The eight quakes indicated, with magnitudes ranging from 4.0 to 6.0 (± 0.5 as always), occurred just where Varotsos had predicted they would. The most violent of them, on October 16, had its epicenter at 37°90' N and 20°90' E (233 km, or 145 mi, west of Athens), and its magnitude was 6 on the Richter scale. The damage was significant: a thousand homes completely destroyed and 17,000 with 70% damage.

On October 31 Professor Varotsos announced that three new tremors would strike the Ionian coast, this time about 275 km (± 20 km), or 171 mi, to the west and southwest of Athens, the strongest with a magnitude of between 4.5 and 5.5 (± 0.5). The shocks occurred as predicted: on October 31 (magnitude 4.9), November 8 (magnitude 5.4) and November 11 (magnitude 5.0), located 230 km [143 mi] west, 170 km [105 mi] southwest, and 270 km [167 mi] west of Athens, respectively.

Four months then passed, during which no signal corresponding to an earthquake of greater than 3.5 magnitude was recorded. During this period, no earthquake with an intensity greater than IV MSK took place in Greece. But on March 1, 1989, two significant SESs were recorded, once again only at Ioannina, and the diagnosis that they yielded was that a 5.4 magnitude earthquake would occur 300 km [186 mi] to the west, and another, with magnitude 5.0, 330 km [205 mi] to the northwest of Athens. They did indeed happen, as predicted, on March 5 and 8.

This series of 17 predictions, concerning three seismic episodes of approximately three weeks' duration each (September, October, and November 1988), followed by a four-month lull and a new episode in March 1989, *all* of which were confirmed in terms of both location and magnitude, shows the value of this method. I had been an absolute skeptic, but by the end of 1988 I had been converted in a few months into the most enthusiastic proponent of the VAN method, and as the experiments continued I could not help thinking about its astonishing possibilities.

But I must repeat and emphasize one thing: the precursor signals cannot be correctly interpreted unless the station receiving them "responds" to that seismic zone. Experience has shown that SESs can be interpreted in terms of epicenter location and magnitude—with almost 100% certainty, it seems—only after a sufficient calibration period for the particular seismic zone + recording station pair. Without this essential calibration the risk of errors remains high; those errors result from an imperfect understanding of how the station in question will respond to signals from the area of the future quake.

First of all—and it took several years to discover this—one must determine whether the seismic electrical signal emitted by a proto-tremor does in fact reach the station or not. For reasons that are undoubtedly geological in nature (faults, underground water tables, or even the type of rock), the telluric signal emanating from a particular seismic zone may or may not arrive at a given VAN station. If it does arrive, we say that *that* station "responds" to *that* zone, and therefore that all the precursor signals coming from it, at least those which indicate a quake of magnitude equal to or greater than that of the first one to be recorded there, will be detected at the station.

In any given seismic region some station sites will respond and others will not. However, those sites may very well respond to other seismic regions. And this phenomenon is an essential criterion for selecting the locations of stations in a network that is intended to monitor all of a particular region: when installing a permanent VAN station, it is not enough to choose a site where the industrial background noise is low enough not to disguise the signal (for example, on the order of a tenth of a millivolt over the 100 meters or 328 feet between the terminals of a dipole). The site must also receive signals from as many potential seismic zones as possible, especially those highly populated regions in which any earthquake, even of modest magnitude, might claim victims.

Varotsos and his colleagues have made another discovery: the fact that a station "responds" to a given zone is not necessarily reciprocal; in other words a station installed in that zone may not receive SESs emanating from the zone in which the responding station is located. In addition, the precursor signals arriving from a particular region may be recorded only on the east-west component of the station, or only the north-south component, or both at once. Another observation: even if two stations "respond" to a given seismic zone, the amplitude of the recorded signal often differs, even when the epicenter is equidistant from the two, because the stations are not equally sensitive to the signals coming from a given region. The degree of sensitivity (the response) of a station to a region depends on the resistivity of each of the two components (east-west and north-south); those resistivity values may differ by as much as two orders of

magnitude. Hence the empirical rule that while the amplitude of an SES of course depends on the magnitude of the
tremor that it is indicating and on its distance, it is also
governed by the sensitivity of the station.

The duration of the precursor signal varies between
half a minute and about two hours. According to Varotsos,
however, there is no correlation between the duration of
the SES and the magnitude of the quake. It is obvious that
the amount of time required to calibrate a given station to
all the zones around it which might produce strong tremors, within a radius that may range from 4 km [2.5 mi] to
200–300 km [125–175 mi], is proportional to the rarity of
the earthquakes within them. It may take 3 to 10 times
longer to do so in a region with infrequent tremors, like
France or the central United States, than in Greece, California, or Japan. Definitive installation of a network may
therefore take decades, since areas which are capable of
delivering a destructive earthquake may nevertheless
remain almost tremor-free for dozens of years.

On the other hand, once a station has been properly
calibrated to one of these unstable regions, in other words,
once the amplitude, polarity, and relationship between
east-west and north-south components of the SESs emitted from it are known, a single station—not three or
four—may be enough to predict the precise location of the
quake indicated by the signal, and its magnitude. This was
demonstrated by the 15 tremors in the autumn of 1988 in
the Gulf of Corinth. But before calibration, before any
experience has been gained from the first shock that
arrives from a given region, it may be impossible to inter-

pret an SES; this explains why some of the earthquakes that occurred in Greece during those first eight years of experimentation were not pinpointed.

Such was the case in 1986 of the destructive earthquake at Kalamata: the relatively nearby stations at Nauplion and Pyrgos (about 50 km or 30 mi away) had not recorded an SES, but the station at Sounion near Athens, 170 km [105 mi] distant, received a very strong signal. Unfortunately, since that station had not yet been calibrated to the southern Peloponnesos, it was impossible to provide any information other than to announce a magnitude 5 earthquake 100 or 150 km [some 60 or 100 mi] from Athens, or a magnitude 6 quake 200 km [125 mi] away. Without calibration, with no opportunity to cross-check with the information that could have been provided by other stations in the network, the azimuth from Athens of that tremor could not be stated or even estimated: the distance, yes, but not its location along that circumference. One last unfortunate paradox was that the recording obtained from the then recently installed station in Kalamata—right at the epicenter—was so chaotic, and the voltage differences were so enormous, that Varotsos and his friends thought that the instruments were malfunctioning, or that industrial currents were intruding, or even that there was some problem with the telephone line. They therefore discounted the information, especially since the other stations in the region had picked up nothing.

Their subsequent analysis of this unpredicted earthquake showed that the wild oscillations of the Kalamata station represented the signals of a major tremor, as can occur right at the epicenter itself. They also realized that the large SES recorded at Sounion came from the seismic focus at Kalamata, so that Sounion is now calibrated in terms of Kalamata. But it was only on further examination that they perceived a third feature: the absence of any precursor signal at Nauplion or Pyrgos.

The explanation of this probably has to do with the geological structure of the region: for example a major fault, perhaps oriented approximately northeast-southwest, may separate the northern and southern portions of the Peloponnesos. Any such fracture in the Earth's crust is always filled with fragments of rock ground up by the fault when it is active; water coming directly from the surface or from underground water tables can then easily infiltrate between these fragments. The result is a kind of aquifer, vertical if the fault is vertical, and otherwise tilted in some way. The water in this aquifer always contains traces of dissolved mineral salts derived from the crushed rocks, and this slightly saline water, which is therefore a much better conductor of electricity than the compact rocks on either side of the fault, constitutes a trap, a curtain through which the telluric currents cannot pass, since its reduced resistance invariably deflects them and diverts them deep into the Earth, taking with them their pre-earthquake message.

It is therefore fairly probable that faults, and perhaps also some ordinary underground aquifers, are what isolate certain stations from certain earthquake-generating zones. The existing VAN network has revealed several non-connections of this type, and one of the problems that must be solved before every point in the territory capable of emitting a precursor signal can be linked, by telluric currents, to one or, even better, two or three stations in the network, is more geological than physical. By undertaking a structural study of the seismogenic zone and the receiving station, it should be fairly easy to detect the "curtains" that may separate them. The network can then be modified on the basis of the information that has progressively been revealed by SESs and tremors. The density of the network will be increased in some places and reduced in others, until it reaches an optimum configuration in which every SES can be detected, and the tremor that it indicates can be predicted exactly.

OTHER APPROACHES

Another approach to the prediction of earthquakes emerged when an American astronomer named Warwick established a correlation between the tremendous 8.7 magnitude earthquake that occurred in Chile on May 20, 1960 and the powerful radio signal that he had detected at his observatory in Hawaii. Since then several astrophysicists and geophysicists have tried to make use of this precursor phenomenon, among them a team led by Gokhberg in the Soviet Union. Although they have confirmed a correlation between radio signals and tremors, as Warwick had demonstrated some thirty years ago, they have not yet succeeded in predicting the location of the earthquake that is being announced. But someone will probably succeed in doing so sooner or later: let us not forget that Milne established a correlation between a telluric signal and its subsequent earthquake back in 1897, and it was not until 1981 that Varotsos and his two colleagues made their first successful prediction based on the interpretation of that signal.

In 1987 I tried unsuccessfully to convince Academician Gokhberg to incorporate the VAN method into his research on the use of radio signals. One year later, however, faced with the unarguable effectiveness of the Greek method, he asked Varotsos to allow some of his assistants to come and learn from him. In France, the VAN network that is being prepared will be supplemented with radio sensors; the additional information collected by these sensors will be used to increase the accuracy of the predictions already provided by the VAN method.

Two pieces of information are still missing, and these could be made available by further processing of the telluric or radio signals: the depth of focus—which, along with the magnitude, would make it possible to estimate the intensity at the epicenter as well as the extent of the area subjected to destructive intensity—and the time period separating the precursor signal from the actual shock.

IV
PROTECTING
OURSELVES
AGAINST
EARTHQUAKES

We have seen that regions with apparently very little seismic activity, such as Switzerland or France, Central Africa or the American Midwest, Germany or Canada, can be jolted just as violently as China, Japan, Greece, Turkey, or the west coast of the Americas. The difference is that in the latter areas destructive earthquakes are relatively frequent, while in the former they are rare. But, I repeat, the only tremor with an estimated magnitude of 9 on the Richter scale occurred in Portugal, a country which is hardly more earthquake-prone than France; and major quakes that undoubtedly exceeded magnitude 8 have occurred in both Spain and Missouri. Because they have happened there before, they will happen there again.

Whether elected officials or civil servants, those responsible for the security of these countries are therefore at fault when they do not take all the necessary preventive measures. Such measures range from predicting earthquakes to organizing effective relief, and include enforcement of earthquake-resistant construction regulations and public education. The pretext usually advanced—that their country has never experienced an earthquake disaster for a century or even more—is false. In France at least, they used to have an excuse for their ignorance about the subject. But since 1960, when I undertook to alert public opinion in this regard, and especially since 1981 when the position of Commissioner for Major Natural Risks was created in the government, that excuse is no longer valid: today, not taking preventive measures is tantamount to refusing assistance to persons in danger.

What I have just said applies to every earthquake-prone region in the world, or almost every one. There are of course some, beginning with Japan, California, Alaska, Monaco, and Yugoslavia, which for two or three decades have been requiring more or less strict compliance with earthquake-resistant construction standards, and educating their people to react intelligently when disaster strikes. When it comes to trying to predict the occurrence of major tremors, only Greece has been doing so effectively since 1981, and Japan and the Rhône/Alpine region are in turn adopting the Greek method. But nowhere in the world has anyone taken the right approach to the difficult problem of effectively organizing relief work.

In 1981 we in France made a good start at addressing this highly complex question rationally. More because of mediocrity than for any legitimate governmental reason, this study was stymied rather than encouraged at the national level. In 1988 an exercise designed to demonstrate our shortcomings in this area—an exercise which moreover had been organized in the context of the Council of Europe and involved an entire *département** (Isère), whose elected officials are particularly aware of the threat represented by poorly organized relief work—was cancelled by the minister "in charge" of public safety. It is obviously a long way from being administratively "in charge" to being ethically responsible.

Mitigation of earthquake risk involves a series of measures, each of which is capable of reducing either the number of victims or the extent and intensity of the destruction, or both: these measures are earthquake-resistant construction, public education, prediction of destructive tremors, and effective organization of relief efforts.

EARTHQUAKE-RESISTANT CONSTRUCTION

First of all, allow me to correct a widespread misconception: earthquake-resistant construction is not expensive. The additional cost involved ranges from nothing to only 8% of the basic structural costs of a building. I am talking of course about a properly constructed building, not the jerry-built shoddy construction that is all too common today, both for individual houses and for more pretentious buildings: just look at the consequences of the tremors at El Asnam and Irpinia in 1980, in Mexico in 1985, in Armenia in 1988, not to mention hundreds of others.

---

* France is divided into 95 administrative districts called *départements*. Isère is one of the larger such districts, covering an area of 8,237 km² (3,200 mi²), about half the size of New Jersey.

Earthquake-resistant construction means obeying a few very simple rules: build on suitable ground (hard bedrock is best, artificial fill is worst); install substantial foundations; use the simplest possible ground plan (square or rectangular); make sure that the load-bearing walls are solidly attached to the foundations; make equally sure that each floor and the roof are also solidly attached to the load-bearing walls; and use materials capable of responding in the best possible way to the abnormal mechanical stresses imposed by earthquakes.

The first principle underlying an earthquake-resistant building is therefore solidity, meaning firm bonding among all the load-bearing elements: foundations, walls, and floors. Thus in a building made of reinforced concrete, the vertical and horizontal reinforcing bars must be securely interconnected. It should also be obvious that the nature of the materials used and their quality are of primary importance.

Earth tremors produce a number of different mechanical stresses; the better they are understood, the better the construction will be. These stresses give rise to movements of varying intensity—horizontal, vertical, or oblique—oriented in a single direction or many, rectilinear, circular, or elliptical, at a variety of frequencies from vibrations to long-wavelength swings. The ground can also give way beneath the building, which is one of the reasons why bedrock is preferable to a friable soil; all too often such soils are saturated with water and thus may liquefy when subjected to vibration, becoming almost instantly incapable of supporting any kind of structure.

The reason is that a soft soil full of water represents a solid continuous phase (each grain of sand in contact with several others) containing a discontinuous liquid phase (microscopic droplets separated from one another). When the soil begins to vibrate the grains move away from one another, and it turns into a continuous liquid phase and a discontinuous solid phase—in other words, a fluid mud into which buildings topple.

Besides choosing a good location, there are really only two satisfactory responses to these various stresses: either make the structure so rigid that its cohesion and solidity allow it to resist disintegration; or give it sufficient elasticity to bend but not break. Elastic materials are more earthquake-resistant than others: wood and steel, of course, but also concrete if it is properly reinforced. Almost no such materials had been used at Spitak in 1988, nor at El Asnam in 1980, nor at Agadir in 1960, nor in many other places.

A Cyclopean structure, intelligently designed and well executed, will also stand up amazingly well to the worst possible tremors, as I have already mentioned with regard to the Inca and pre-Inca buildings at Machu Picchu—and I should have included pre-Hellenic structures at sites such as Mycenae, and Etruscan walls. The Imperial palace in Tokyo and the Cyclopean walls surrounding it, built long ago using a technique very similar to that of the Incas and Etruscans, has withstood earthquakes extremely well. These walls consist of enormous blocks of stone cut into prismatic shapes, with a variety of dimensions and (especially important) angles, shaped with such precision that they fit together with absolutely no need for mortar. This configuration of trapezoidal blocks, each weighing up to several tons, has in some cases proved over the centuries to be an astonishingly effective earthquake-proofing system in regions that are often rocked by very severe tremors.

Less aesthetically pleasing but today incomparably less expensive, modern buildings—whether made of high-quality concrete or steel frames with glass cladding—are also very strong. There are certain prerequisites, of course: the steel must be of the requisite quality, elementary principles must be observed, the engineering calculations must be performed correctly, and the building must be constructed by competent and honest builders. Such is not always the case.

Single-family homes can be constructed to earthquake-resistant standards simply by applying the few simple principles listed above. However, the construction of very tall structures, hospitals, factories, schools, auditoriums, bridges, docks, aqueducts, warehouses, telephone exchanges, dams, etc. requires stupendous know-how and a great deal of caution. We in France—a country whose backwardness in terms of earthquake risk abatement is enormous and, to put it bluntly, quite scandalous—can nonetheless be proud of the quality and breadth of our specialists' earthquake-resistant engineering capabilities. In some fifteen years, their abilities have reached such a high level that, not satisfied with having assimilated all the knowledge that has slowly been accumulated since the beginning of the century by engineers on America's west coast and in Japan, they have uncovered new information. Thus it was a French team that published, in 1985, the world's very first (and so far its only) complete treatise on earthquake-resistant engineering.

In a little book such as this one, I obviously cannot attempt to summarize the 1,100 pages, written by more than 100 authors, of this monumental work entitled *Génie parasismique* [Earthquake-resistant engineering], or its 11 sections and 78 chapters. But even a simple list of these 11 sections and some of the more important chapters might interest any engineers who happen to be reading this book (other readers may, in good conscience, skip this section).

The book begins with an introduction which discusses planning for earthquake-resistant construction, then continues with general seismology and seismogenesis, a study of small-scale movements, an evaluation of seismic hazards, accounting for seismic effects on soils, dynamic calculations, soil/structure interactions, compensating for seismic effects on industrial equipment, and how seismic risks are actually dealt with.

Here are the titles of some of the principal chapters:

- Specific characteristics of seismic action
- Seismic data processing
- Ground displacements during an earthquake
- Time distribution of aftershocks
- Seismic instrumentation
- Various effects resulting from earthquakes, and methods of measuring them

85

- Seismotectonic map of France
- Scientific and engineering approaches to seismic engineering analysis
- Small-scale zoning
- Site effects
- Microzoning
- Behavior of soils under cyclic loading
- Behavior of powdery environments
- Free-field response of a soil profile
- Evaluating liquefaction risks
- Damping
- Modal analysis in structural calculations
- Dynamic analysis of structures
- Response spectra and accelerograms
- Characteristics of reinforced-concrete structures
- Reinforced-concrete framework and masonry lining
- Prestressing in seismic zones
- Dimensioning metal structures
- Lessons learned from earthquakes
- Earthquake-resistant dam design
- Walls and retaining structures
- Bridges
- Earthquake-resistant supports
- Earthquake resistance of buried conduits, tunnels, and underground structures
- Protecting essential public-works and industrial equipment
- Fluid–structure interactions
- Earthquake-related pipework calculations

- Primary cooling circuits in nuclear power plants
- Seismic analysis of fast nuclear reactors
- Models and methods for designing mechanical equipment
- Electrical equipment in distribution grids
- Urban planning and earthquake risks
- Legal aspects

etc.

And this represents only a bit more than half the chapters in the book!

EDUCATING THE PUBLIC

During an earthquake as in almost any other dangerous situation, it is possible to save one's own life, to save other people's lives, and to reduce the risk of serious injury; in other words, to escape the worst. To do so one must understand the potential danger, then know how to react when it presents itself, and finally maintain enough composure to use that knowledge.

Keeping a cool head is the most important thing. Anyone who is not abnormally nervous and has a minimum of self-control can do it: desire is enough, but training helps. It is possible, for example, in only a few minutes, to calm a child or anyone who has been terrified witless—something I learned by experience during a prolonged bombing raid. It is therefore unquestionably possible to teach people, while everything is normal, not to succumb to panic when a make-believe danger occurs, and then progressively train them to remain calm in the face of real danger.

An understanding of the danger is just as important, and is not difficult to acquire. Let us take the example of prospective automobile drivers. We teach them to put on the emergency brake when they park the car and release it when they drive off, to fit into the space between two parked cars, and other trivia—necessary, of course, but minor. What we *should* teach them is not to brake when an obstacle suddenly appears in front of a driver going 50 mph, but to avoid it; we would then have incomparably fewer traffic injuries. The best reaction, after all, is not to slam on the brakes, but to steer slightly to the left or to the right—and composure is an essential element in making the choice—to avoid the obstacle. But one must also be aware that at relatively high speeds, in order to prevent a pileup, it is best to accelerate at the same time: quite the opposite of hitting the brakes.

Another case in point. Most victims of fires these days do not burn to death, they asphyxiate: they are killed by the organic vapors, some of them chlorinated or fluorinated, during combustion of the innumerable plastics which have now replaced wood, leather, stone, wool, plant fibers, and metals in construction, furniture, and appliances. If a fire breaks out, the idea is therefore not to run thoughtlessly towards some exit, but to try to get there while keeping one's respiratory passages below, not on the same level as, the toxic gases; since these are hot and therefore lighter than air, they rise. In other words, head for the emergency exit with your head down, or on all fours, crawling under the lethal fumes.

The same applies to earthquakes. As in any confrontation, the first prerequisite is to stay cool. The next thing to realize is that any earthquake, no matter how powerful, does not *instantly* demolish buildings or trigger landslides (which, if you do not react correctly, might break your bones or bury you). An earthquake takes seconds or sometimes tens of seconds to cause disastrous collapses. Those few seconds may be enough for you to seek safety, either by getting out of the building if you are on the ground floor or one of the lower floors (although you should never venture into the elevator, a terrible trap in any earthquake) or by shielding yourself as best you can: under a solid piece of furniture, under a bed, in the corner formed by two load-bearing walls, in any case far away from windows and mirrors which can shatter and cut like razors, and also away from hanging items that might come loose, heavy furniture that might tip over or even slide over and gore you like a bull.

You must also know that if, despite all your precautions, you find yourself buried under debris but are still alive and conscious, you absolutely must remain calm. Panic will drain your psychological and physical strength, reducing the time you can endure without food or water until help arrives. I know of one extreme case in which several young, healthy men were dead in a few hours, because they thought all hope was lost and they panicked. And this was not even under piles of debris but out in the open—admittedly at night, in bad weather, and during an eruption in the crater of Piton de la Fournaise—but under circumstances where nothing, except loss of self-control and the exhaustion that results from it, presented any imminent danger. I know of far too many other examples in which people died who would have survived if they had displayed more strength of character. Alain Bombard mentions many of them; he has studied them, and they inspired his extraordinary survival technique which has saved countless shipwreck victims over the last thirty years, a technique based on calm and understanding. And there are cases in which victims buried during a destructive earthquake have been rescued ten or even twelve days later, as happened in Mexico in 1985.

A major earthquake is always followed by less violent tremors called aftershocks; but even these can be destructive because they sometimes bring down buildings that withstood the main shock but were weakened by it. This situation is of concern both to survivors and to rescue workers.

For some time now, certain countries that are often struck by killer earthquakes have been facing up to the responsibility of educating people about what to do when the ground starts shaking. They realized very quickly that the most effective way to make a deep impression on the population is to talk to the children. Advertising people are well aware of this fact, and exploit it when they are trying to sell not only candy or toys, but also such unchildlike merchandise as gasoline or computers. To get this kind of message across, for example what to do in case of an earthquake, the best approach is therefore through the schools, using methods such as comic-strip posters.

The results of this policy in Japan have already been very satisfactory. In France, towards the end of the period when I was responsible for mitigating major risks, I shamelessly imitated both the Japanese and the Greeks, who had given me some of their posters; I had my own versions of them drawn by Piem, a well-known and excellent cartoonist. I extracted from a colleague in charge of national education a promise that they would be printed, distributed, and posted in every school in the most seismically active areas of the country. But some particularly zealous bureaucrat saw to it that nothing happened before the elections of March 1986, which sent us all back to private life. I have no idea what happened to the poster project, but as I write these lines, two governments and three Ministers of National Education have followed the one who agreed to implement the program, and our children still do not know what to do if an earthquake strikes. As a consequence, their parents and teachers also do not know.

There are many, indeed far too many others who, although they have no excuse not to know, are in the same position, from the minister responsible for rescue operations and the *préfets** in charge of managing them in each *département*, to the majority of our basic service personnel: firefighters and emergency medical service teams,

---

* A *préfet* is the administrative official in charge of a *département* of France, approximately equivalent to an American state governor.

among others. I will come back to this subject, but it is worth repeating things when they are very important. And in this case they are.

ORGANIZING RELIEF WORK AFTER A MAJOR EARTHQUAKE

Once the earthquake prevention system has been adopted by all the various countries at risk, and once the essential calibrations that I mentioned (between seismic zones and earthquake-signal recording stations) have finally made it possible to issue timely alerts to the proper authorities and populations involved, the number of victims will be reduced to the point where it will be almost easy to organize effective relief work.

Until then, millions of people will lose their lives and millions more will be seriously injured: many of them could survive and would suffer only minor injuries if relief efforts were properly prepared and organized. But where a major disaster is concerned, that relief work is never effective, not in France or anywhere else.

I will discuss France because I know it best and because I am aware of the strong cards that we hold. But I also know our weaknesses in this regard, because for five years, through three governments during the period from 1981 to 1986, I was responsible for disaster relief. The organization of effective rescue work plays an essential part in such relief: I said as much many times when I held that office, and I delivered the message in writing to the President of France, who had my report published in the *Journal Officiel** so that the information would be passed on to the civil service and to elected officials. Five years have passed since then, and practically nothing has been done to try to improve the situation. But the more time passes, the closer we are getting to the next disaster. If no one has even taken on this responsibility, who will then take the blame for the number of victims?

The paradox is glaring: we live in a country where assistance in the event of an accident, even a serious one, is almost always provided with great expertise by fire-fighters and emergency medical personnel, as well as by all the other participants who are generally alerted: police, *gendarmes*,** ambulances, private physicians, nurses, and non-governmental organizations such as the Red Cross. But when a true disaster strikes, the organization of this relief work is deplorable, as drills have repeatedly demonstrated.

There are two reasons for this. It appears that the authorities have not yet understood that the difference between an emergency and a disaster is not just the dimensions of the event, but also, because of its magnitude, the type of response required: just as an accident is not just a large-scale incident, a disaster is much more complex than an exceptionally major accident. What is more, when it comes to disasters these authorities lack

---

* Approximately equivalent to the *Congressional Record*.
** Part militia and part police, organized at both the *département* and national levels.

experience, they lack the imagination that would help reduce the negative effects of their inexperience, and they lack modesty.

There are many differences between an accident and a disaster, but the most important of them, which I will mention first, is what military doctors (experts on the subject) call a "large number of wounded." This large number exists whenever a physician specializing in this type of situation—and they are rare—finds himself forced to treat five wounded people simultaneously, by himself. In a serious earthquake, each doctor must deal with dozens, sometimes even hundreds of survivors.

The second characteristic that distinguishes disasters from mere accidents is a more or less total breakdown of the logistical infrastructure: roads, railways, airports, harbors, power lines, telephone cables and exchanges, water mains, gas ducts, hospitals, radio and television relays; not to mention the government, its offices, its files, and now its computers. This disintegration can be so severe as to prevent any movement of rescue operations, heavy equipment especially, but also of people, who find it just as difficult to overcome obstacles such as downed bridges, blocked roads and—once they finally reach the zone around the epicenter—streets filled with the rubble of collapsed buildings, all of which will always tend to slow down rescue efforts.

Any delay will raise the number of victims: the effectiveness of any rescue operation depends above all on its speed, because the percentage of buried victims who die rises almost exponentially with each hour that ticks away. The most severely wounded will succumb first, as will those with the most fragile nerves and those whose morale is not solid enough to sustain them in the inhuman conditions into which they have suddenly been thrust. Then, one after another, the often less seriously affected survivors, who could not be reached in time, will start dying.

To reach them is indeed difficult and sometimes impossible. The factors involved include both the initial distance separating rescuers from victims, and the obstacles—physical ones, to be sure, but sometimes simply administrative ones as well that the rescuers must overcome. Success also depends, of course, on the rescuers' competence: their calling is a demanding one, and experience is as much a part of it as training, courage, and initiative. Reaching the survivors also depends on the kind of equipment available, both to find the victims and to extract them from their prisons of slabs and girders, iron and concrete, jumbled and piled-up debris. But the speed of rescue operations also depends on logistical organization, in other words everything having to do with telecommunications, transportation, supplies, police, and the civilian and military rescue squads, whose arrival must be controlled so that they do not interfere with one another. Interactions should be managed so that they are complementary and thus effective, not anarchic (or even competitive) and therefore ineffective, as all too often they are.

The first important factor governing survivor mortality is therefore the initial distance that separates rescuers from victims. That much is obvious. To minimize the death toll, every possible resource must be applied to reducing that distance. One way is to train lots of physicians in specialized disaster medicine and, to the extent possible, station them appropriately around the country. When I was responsible for major risk mitigation, this idea led me to develop the teaching of disaster medicine in France: the greater the number of such specialists, the greater the chances that some of them will be near or even at the affected site, and the shorter the time span between the collapse of a building and the provision of care to the injured. The result: chances for survival will be considerably increased, or at least injuries will not be aggravated.

Good organization also presupposes that an increased number of specialists in the detection and extrication of surviving victims can be distributed around the country. The best solution would be to provide specialized training for firefighters, preparing them for specific tasks. In this context it would obviously be most appropriate for senior officials, those responsible for both public safety and firefighting, to finally approach the risk of an earthquake disaster in France with the earnest attention it deserves. It would be desirable if they could do so before the next destructive earthquake, and not end up, as so often happens, taking preventive measures *after* the disaster.

Every disastrous earthquake, without exception, has shown that most of the victims who were pulled from the rubble alive were rescued within minutes after the buildings collapsed, in other words by people who were on the spot or in the vicinity and who, having escaped being buried themselves, went to work right away. Rescuers coming from farther away—nearby towns and areas, then more distant regions and adjacent countries, finally from distant nations—arrive later and later, hours or even days after the destructive tremor, and can therefore save very few people... sometimes even nobody at all.

Governments wanting to provide real protection for their citizens, as well as the higher officials who are supposed to be representing them, should therefore work to increase the percentage of potential rescuers who are skilled in the various techniques of extricating victims, and the number of physicians and nurses expert in providing this kind of care. These ideas have been slowly gaining acceptance over the last half-dozen years: too slowly, in my opinion, but the situation is still far better than what it was in this area less than even ten years ago, when to tell the truth almost nothing existed.

However, even when these measures have actually been implemented and one can count on a certain number of specialists able to intervene immediately and thus rescue a significantly greater proportion of survivors, these few specialists on the scene will obviously never be able to deal with the enormous problems that must be addressed once the initial phase is over. Those who have never seen a large-scale catastrophe with their own eyes cannot even conceive of these problems: because any disaster is so large and so complex, it demands a strategy on a national scale, as well as flexible tactics to suit each local situation.

Strategy and tactics are military terms, and of course whenever a nation—no matter what its political system— is struck by a large-scale disaster, the government immediately calls in the armed forces. A natural disaster does indeed represent, for society and for those who govern it, a kind of aggression which differs only in its details from an enemy attack. The earthquake which converted me, a scientific researcher specializing in volcanology, into a disaster mitigation specialist occurred on May 20, 1960, in southern Chile. In a few moments, it devastated a region some 200 miles wide and 600 miles long; an area half the size of France. The aggressions of Nature are as serious as the worst that humans can devise, and, with the exception of nuclear war, incomparably more sudden.

But no government, be it totalitarian or democratic, military or civilian, right-wing or left, whether it oversees an "industrialized" or a "developing" country, no matter whether the nation is rich or poor, guided by leaders of exceptional intelligence or oppressed by gangsters who have grabbed the reins of power (or even both at once)— no government has as yet understood that it must defend itself against natural aggression with the same resolve that it applies (or tries to apply) to attacks from its neighbors. And the attacks of Nature are inevitable, while the others are never more than hypothetical.

Every government devotes the largest portion of its budget to national defense, but none of them deigns to spend even a hundredth as much to defend itself against natural disasters! This explains our total inability to respond to such disasters in the way we should. The explanation for this has far more to do with the lobbying pressure applied to politicians—whose greatest virtue is not courage—than with ignorance. There's no person so deaf as the one who doesn't want to hear.

Yet it is much less difficult and incomparably less expensive to defend oneself against natural threats than against military attacks, and an investment in this sort of protection would be a most profitable way to reduce the losses, of both property and lives, inflicted on us by natural disasters. What we have not had so far are leaders with enough vision to understand this, leaders concerned more with the public interest than with their personal interests, leaders with enough courage to stand up to the pressure groups which usually have the upper hand.

In France, after a period of a few years during which the government appeared to have decided to initiate a serious disaster mitigation program, it now seems once again to be confronting the threat of destructive earthquakes with the same head-in-the-sand policy that had prevailed prior to May 1981: it is not enforcing earthquake-resistant construction regulations in threatened areas, it is doing nothing to educate the people involved, it is not doing much to improve disaster relief planning, and it is doing even less to try to predict earthquakes.

THE ROLE OF THE MILITARY

Relief work, one of the three legs of the mitigation triad—prediction and prevention being the other two—should therefore be organized so that relief work is effective even when, following a *Blitzkrieg* attack by Nature, the entire economic and administrative infrastructure is at least partially destroyed.

What follows, which might serve as a starting point for the farsighted and courageous leader of whom I dream, is the result of more than 25 years of reflection, to which I have devoted even more effort in the last decade: it is based on my personal experience, on a serious analysis of many major disasters, and on my conversations with competent people.

One fact must be understood from the outset: always and without exception, as soon as a problem develops beyond a certain threshold and becomes a disaster, the government calls in the armed forces to help deal with the situation. Why? Because no matter what the form of government, only the armed forces have enough people, trained to obey and carry out the orders issued to them, who are operational around the clock: military hierarchies were created for precisely those ends. Furthermore, only an army has the quantity of equipment needed to conduct rescue operations and care for survivors: telecommunications; ground, air and sea transportation; bulldozers, backhoes, hoisting gear, power saws, explosives, field hospitals, mobile kitchens, tents, cots, stockpiles of medications, blankets, food... and heaven knows what else. Not making use of the armed forces means losing time, doing without resources, and therefore multiplying the death toll.

A second fact that must be understood is that despite the assistance of the armed forces, and no matter what the quality—usually excellent—and quantity—always completely inadequate—of the civilian personnel involved in organizing relief efforts, those efforts are either inefficient or completely ineffectual. Why? Because the human resources mobilized for relief work do not have the knowledge they need to carry out this kind of operation. After all, military forces are not usually deployed to keep people from getting killed: quite the opposite. Military training puts very little emphasis on the techniques or the attitudes needed for relief work, and when soldiers, tank crews, mountain commandos, pilots, sailors, or paratroopers are called in, it is therefore unreasonable to expect more from their participation than from that of the average citizen. Hence the lack of effectiveness despite the great numbers of personnel and amount of equipment available. In this area as in every other, attitude is all-important. There are exceptions in France, and I know of nothing comparable in other countries: they are our two civil defense intervention units, the Paris firefighter brigade and the fireboat battalion in Marseilles.

The obvious conclusion to be drawn from these two observations—the need to call in the armed forces but also the fact that their effectiveness is nonetheless quite inadequate—is that the best approach, in every country that has not yet done so (which is almost all of them), would be to train certain military units in rescue and relief work. If such units already exist, as they do in France, then create more of them.

However, this will never be anything more than applying a Band-Aid to a severely injured body. Because essentially what is lacking are not specialized units, but a structure capable of both integrating as harmoniously as possible all the civilian and military entities, whether specialized or not, that will be participating in the relief effort; and coordinating their work in both time and space. In time, by first of all controlling the arrival of each unit on the scene and then assigning them in rotation to the various work sites; and in space so as ensure optimum coverage of the entire disaster area. These forces must also be made to work so that their various specializations complement each other, to avoid overstaffing some areas and short-changing others.

What one always finds, whether at the scene of a real disaster or at a drill, is an anarchic juxtaposition or superposition of efforts, some performed well and others not, but with no cooperation among the participating groups, no liaison, no hierarchy, no strategy. On the contrary, all too often the already reduced effectiveness of such an agglomeration of helping hands becomes further degraded by the baneful effect of inter-service, interregional and even international rivalries, whipped up over twenty-five years by media attention and the sordid interests that underlie it: at present, these enormous relief operations are characterized by an obvious lack of understanding, good will, and willingness to cooperate. Sometimes the situation becomes downright hateful, and the bad feeling is as all-pervasive as the stench of corpses. I speak from experience, and I have chosen my words carefully.

The competition, the vanity, the desire to be seen, to draw attention to oneself—all of it exacerbated by the presence of cameras and microphones—are thus partly responsible for the shortcomings which reduce even further a level of effectiveness that was never very satisfactory in the first place. But the major reason for this regrettable state of affairs is, I repeat, the absence of any structure capable of managing the plethora of diverse people and resources which pour onto the scene of a disaster. Whether the operations are directed by civilians, as in France or Italy, or by the military, as in Mexico, Colombia, or Cameroon, the result is always deplorable: the ratio between "resources applied" and "lives saved" is distressingly low.

When the military is involved, order is paramount and is quickly re-established, but since life counts for little, the bulldozers are often put into action too soon, levelling the ruins and restoring a dignified and presentable appearance with no thought for the victims buried under those ruins, who might have survived for another two weeks. And when civilians are in charge, chaos reigns from start to finish; that is more than enough to explain the inefficiency.

Obviously I am most familiar with the situation in France, but *mutatis mutandis*, the same conditions exist elsewhere. In France it is the *préfet*, representing the central government in the *département* or region affected, who is responsible by law for overseeing relief work. In the event of a major accident, assuming the firefighters and emergency medical service teams are not overwhelmed by the magnitude of the event, the *préfets* perform their tasks extremely well, provided their personal qualities are up to it. But when a true disaster occurs, they do not stand a chance.

The principal reason is that they do not possess the hierarchical links that would allow them to transmit their instructions to the people working on the scene: those already at the sites of the catastrophe trying to find, extricate, and care for the survivors; or those who are attempting to reach the disaster area through traffic jams, impassable roads, and rubble. They do not possess these hierarchical links because there are no structures which can interconnect entities as disparate as the firefighters, the military, the emergency medical services, the Red Cross, the Red Crescent, *Médecins du Monde* [Doctors of the World], *Médecins sans Frontières* [Doctors Without Borders], and other relief organizations, as well as private physicians, the *gendarmes*, the national and municipal police, individual relief workers, not to mention elected officials. The situation becomes even more complicated with rivalries among different firefighting units, different military units, EMS teams from different *départements*, between associations, between… you name it.

It would be easy, if the need arose, to establish an orderly relationship among military units, since they all belong to the same armed forces and are therefore part of an effective hierarchical system. It is almost impossible to do so, however, for any of the other organizations involved, for instance the firefighters: except for the *military* squad in Paris and the *military* battalion in Marseilles, the only hierarchy they have is within each of these entities, with no way of getting the unit next door to cooperate. Hence the anarchy that reigns in France when simulated earthquake drills are held or, even worse, when large-scale forest fires actually occur: what will happen when a real earthquake strikes? When the roads actually are cut off, when there is no more telephone service or transportation, when the people in charge of performing the various tasks at the various levels set forth in the infamous ORSEC (major civil emergency) plans will not be at their posts and ready to carry out instructions immediately, as they are during a drill, but instead—even if they have escaped the disaster and if their concern for themselves or their families allows them to do so—will be incapable of performing those tasks because they have absolutely no way of communicating? The *préfets* will then find themselves in a simply impossible situation. The same will apply to the government, and to the very highest officials of the Republic.

Lawmakers have made no provision for this situation. They have not foreseen the chaos unleashed by a major disaster, and they have legislated in complete ignorance of the facts. But that seems to be standard procedure when it comes to major risks, as confirmed by a recent law mandating the preparation of risk exposure maps (REMs) in each municipality in France that could conceivably be struck by a natural disaster. These large-scale maps are supposed to divide the municipality into three areas: red, so highly threatened that any construction in it will be prohibited; white, where the risk is assumed to be zero; and between the two, blue, where construction will be permitted provided certain precautions are taken.

Are these lawmakers aware that the line separating such zones is extremely difficult to define, even for a "well-behaved" disaster like gradually rising flood waters? That it is *impossible* to define for large landslides, exceptional avalanches, and sudden floods? And that where earthquakes are concerned, that line can be 5 to 25 miles *wide*? This renders the much-vaunted (and expensive) REMs completely meaningless. Dreamed up in some National Assembly* office by elected officials and official representatives more preoccupied with elections or their personal careers than with competence in the area of natural risks, these blueprints will never be anything but sources of interminable, costly, and useless disputes.

The lawmaker who decided one day that each *préfet* should direct relief operations in his or her *département* or region in the event of a disaster was just as well-informed about the complexity of this sort of situation as the one who invented the REMs a few years later. But the poor *préfets* are helpless. Nor can they get out from under the ORSEC plans, even more infamous than the REMs and of even more dubious usefulness. The word "plan" usually suggests an orderly sequence of decisions to be made and operations to be undertaken in order to reach a goal, in this case public safety. But the ORSEC "plans" do not fit this definition at all, since they are hardly more than lists: lists of people and organizations with addresses and telephone numbers, and lists of equipment; lists accompanied by instructions which in my opinion are just as likely to help the *préfets* fight their battles as those which, in May 1940,

* Lower house of the French Parliament.

some of us refused to follow in order to put up our best possible resistance to the Wehrmacht.

The lawmaker who decided that the *préfets* should organize relief work did not think about the essential difference between managing a region in normal times and managing it during a serious crisis: the *École Nationale d'Administration** does not prepare its students, nor does it claim to prepare them to command troops on a battlefield, any more than the *École Militaire*** tries to prepare *its* people to run a *département* in peacetime. By making *préfets* responsible for mobilizing, instructing, and commanding the troops which will have to combat the effects of a major earthquake, the lawmaker made a mistake equivalent to placing a commando general in charge of a small town in peacetime.

Some of the *préfets* with whom I have shared these thoughts have retorted that it would not in fact be they themselves giving the orders when faced with a natural catastrophe, but their local civil defense directors. Unfortunately, these high officials have almost no experience with this type of emergency, nor do they have the technical and psychological training that is essential for managing it properly. Since their position in the chain of command gives them less authority than the *préfet* over the great variety of personnel that would be involved, any illusions about the effectiveness of relief efforts when future earthquakes occur are bound to end in tears.

---

* *The* state-run graduate school of business administration: the fast track to a government career.
** Officer training academy for all of the French armed forces.

107

In reality the situation will never be acceptably resolved until certain statutes have been repealed and replaced by other, more judicious legislation based on the findings I have discussed above, which I will summarize again: the government always calls in the armed forces as soon as the scale of a disaster exceeds a certain threshold; despite military assistance, relief efforts are always much too ineffective; neither the *préfets* nor their staff, lacking specialized knowledge in this very specific field and lacking a well-ordered structure, can properly direct the various participants, nor get them to cooperate in order to improve effectiveness; they are not in a position to receive information readily or answer any questions which those participants might have; this lack of hierarchical structure prevents them not only from accommodating the various participants in the joint relief effort and helping them become integrated, but also from transmitting messages and instructions, upward, downward or laterally.

I must insist on this point again: there exists only one institution which not only possesses such a structure, but is also prepared to place it at the nation's disposal at any time; and that is the armed forces. Except in time of war (which now seems a very remote possibility), it can at any moment divert the necessary personnel to a task of such universal benefit as the one we are discussing here. Because of their hierarchical structure, only the armed forces can easily fill the one essential gap that we face: the lack of a structure capable of managing the immense problems presented by relief work in the event of a major disaster.

You might reply that in all too many countries where the armed forces are in charge of such responsibilities, matters are no better than elsewhere, or in fact even worse. That is quite true, as I have already clearly stated; but in those countries the opportunities offered by the military are poorly exploited, most of all because the armed forces have not received the necessary instruction and have not been prepared for this type of activity. Neither the general staff nor the NCOs nor the soldiers have received the specific and essential training that will turn them, from the top of the hierarchical pyramid to the bottom, into true rescuers. When called upon, the armed forces condescend to temporarily set aside their mission, which is to defend the national territory (and in some countries the established order), and do something else. They do so with their characteristic attitude, which is to present a well-defined and rigorous image of themselves (of the unit to which they belong, the armed forces in general, and ultimately the nation). However, trained psychologically to defend these ideals and technically to fight against an enemy (*a priori* a foreign one), they are in no way prepared to search for survivors or to assist a miserable population that has been plunged into misfortune: as far as the military is concerned, it is normally the medical units which deal with those sorts of problems; "normally" meaning, in this case, in wartime: In peacetime, say the generals, that is a job for civilians.

Whether it is our wicked stepmother Earth that is making war on us, or our fellow human beings who happen to speak another language or worship another god, no matter: war is war. A lightning assault, to be sure, extremely brief but also extremely destructive and deadly. The armed forces' medical teams are the units best prepared to respond appropriately to the sudden influx of wounded: contusions, fractures, burns, gas inhalation, eviscerations, electrocutions, asphyxiations, multiple traumas, shock, and more. They can respond to them, and do so extremely well. Unfortunately, the other units making up the armed forces, who might be capable of providing effective services in other relief arenas, have not been at all sensitized to do so: from the corps of engineers with its skills and equipment for earthmoving, hoisting, and cutting, to the transport and telecommunications units, including all the services capable of transporting, sheltering, housing, and feeding survivors, none of these entities has been prepared for the complex and difficult task of searching for and locating survivors in the ruins, pulling them out, feeding them, housing them, and helping them overcome their confusion.

To improve this situation, the relevant civilian authorities, primarily the government, must first be induced to take the seismic threat seriously and stop merely paying lip-service to it; then the military authorities must be persuaded to think about the fundamental role they will have to play in future disasters. Everyone must understand the urgent need to modify military training so that soldiers' psychological attitudes develop at the same pace as their technical expertise.

Then it will be easier to assemble the structure designed first to accommodate and then to assign all the rescuers pouring into a disaster area, and to coordinate their efforts for maximum efficiency. The skeleton of the structure will resemble a pyramid. All the rescuers will take up their positions among the rafters, tie-beams, crosspieces, corner angles, purlins, sills, longitudinal girders, angle rafters, braces, struts, and beams of this framework, from the firefighting brigades to the engineering corps, including EMS personnel, rescue squads, non-governmental organizations (of which the Red Cross is the best known), and military units that are not relief specialists but have been brought in to assist either with physical labor or with their equipment, from helicopters to mobile kitchens.

At the top of this pyramid the general will control the entire organization; officers of decreasing rank will form the chain of command down to the base. From colonels to corporals, every rank will specialize in different and often complex tasks, which everyone must perform simultaneously in order to minimize the death toll: communications, extricating people from the rubble, caring for survivors, information, medical care for victims, maintaining security and order, providing food, etc.

Within this framework of these military specialists whose rank structure is evident to all the participants, the rescuers—both civilian and military—will be able to concentrate on a single objective: saving lives. The often scandalous rivalries, incomprehensible competitiveness, the indolence and even indifference sometimes exhibited—all that will now be eliminated or at least greatly reduced by the vigilance and the energetic, decisive action of this cadre of highly motivated, highly competent, and highly specialized military personnel committed to this mission, which today does not exist.

Another enormous advantage of this pyramidal organizational and control framework will be to minimize the traffic jams, road blockages, and delays which mean more serious injuries and more deaths. One of the great difficulties rescue authorities must overcome, after all, is that of distributing, in time and space, what might be called the "power buildup" of the relief effort. In actuality, even during drills (that is, under incomparably less hostile conditions than those of an actual disaster), this buildup is very poorly managed; in mountainous areas in particular, convoy traffic jams, overloaded access routes, and endless hours of delay can ultimately reduce the effectiveness of these poorly managed efforts to almost zero.

When an intense earthquake occurs in a populated area relief forces must converge towards its epicenter from the most distant *départements*, from neighboring countries, and even from certain faraway countries, and this buildup must be organized very rigorously. Otherwise there will be a superabundance of resources in one place and shortages elsewhere; superabundance means congestion, and that means loss of efficiency. Shortages, of course, are even worse.

Those responsible for this organizational task, in other words those at the top of the pyramid, must be capable of very rapidly assessing the severity of the situation in the various affected regions, the condition of the communications routes leading to them, the strength—in terms of both people and equipment—of the various relief units that might be heading for the area, the professional quality of each, and lastly the time that it would take each one to reach the area. They must take into account distance and obstacles, such as impassable roads, downed bridges, etc., but also the difficulties resulting from the exodus of survivors and, too often, from the flood of onlookers, self-professed experts (or experts with genuine credentials who would nevertheless be useless for the first few days), journalists, politicians, geologists, geophysicists, engineers, and sociologists, not to mention the usual criminal elements.

To make a sound assessment of these highly complex factors, those in charge must, at the very outset, have a clear understanding of the capabilities of each relief column as well as of the itineraries they should be told to take and, on each route, the new difficulties caused by the disaster. They must have the best possible overview of the situation in the affected region so as to distribute relief resources as they arrive in order ultimately to achieve the maximum possible effectiveness.

The difficulty in sizing up the situation on the ground is on a par with the difficulty in reaching the devastated area. Today, fortunately, the helicopter and the television camera have multiplied a thousandfold or more the speed and accuracy of information flow in this field: the organizing official, in radio contact with the helicopter crew that is making observations and taking pictures, sees on a television screen everything that the crew sees, hears their comments, and transmits to them questions and suggestions, all of which makes for exceptionally productive reconnaissance. Supplemented by information from ground-based teams already on the scene, this data gives the general staff an idea of the situation that is precise enough to allow optimal organization of the "power buildup" strategy.

This pyramidal framework must be made up of true relief specialists, not bureaucrats passing themselves off as experts. The more on-site experience these specialists have with major disasters, the greater their knowledge of rescue work will be, and the better they will know how to organize it. At the present state of affairs, I would recommend recruiting these people essentially from public-safety units: first because of their professional experience in that field, and second because the very mission of these units gives them all the necessary flexibility.

Firefighting units, for example, whether military or civilian, are continuously on call to intervene in the event of an accident or disaster in the city whose safety they are monitoring. It is only very exceptionally that they will reduce the number of people taking on that responsibility in order to go elsewhere and give assistance to colleagues who have been forced, by the magnitude of a disaster—derailment, forest fire, large explosion or conflagration—to ask for such aid. In the event of a major disaster, of course, many towns and *départements* will dispatch backup teams taken from their own firefighting personnel. But these are only isolated operations, lasting a day or a few days at most, while the pyramidal framework must be in place permanently, 365 days a year.

If it were not, the time lost in setting it up once the disaster struck would inevitably be several hours. But the most important factor governing the effectiveness of rescue work is speed. Rounding up the members of the pyramid, if they are not part of a dedicated organization, will use up precious hours (precious to those who are sincerely concerned about human lives), and will add to the inevitable difficulties encountered whenever people are mobilized from different groups and locations. The events of 1939 and 1940 sadly demonstrated this, in a context that was only superficially different.

Moreover, it is essential that this structure be on continuous alert, just like the armed forces that are ready to respond instantly to enemy aggression. It has now been fifty years since France has suffered any such attack, and there is little probability that it will experience one soon. In no way does this preclude our national defense from being always ready; and every year successive governments, like every President of the Republic one after the other, have granted those forces the funding necessary for their mission. It would be somewhat astonishing indeed if a government, once its eyes were opened to the considerable threat of an earthquake—which, unlike an enemy attack, is inescapable—did not allocate to this indispensable organizational structure the legal, technical, and financial resources which would allow it to save its citizens' lives when the time came.

THE ROLE OF GOVERNMENT

To whom will this unit report, and which civilian authority will bear the supreme responsibility for this entire organization, overseeing the specialized general who will technically control it? In France it has always been the Minister of the Interior who has taken on this responsibility. When I say "taken on," I am using the term loosely: just recall the eruption of La Soufrière on the island of Guadeloupe in 1976. Seventy thousand people were displaced for four months for no reason, a non-stop air lift operated between France and the Caribbean for this entire period, and hundreds of firefighters from the Paris brigade were sent to Guadeloupe (to put out the volcano?). Hundreds of millions of francs were wasted, thousands of poor families were reduced to destitution, the island's economy was ruined... but who remembers all this? Were the ministers responsible ever called to account before the nation for these mistakes?

The ministers responsible for such mistakes, the gross errors committed both in disaster prevention and in organizing the relief work that follows disasters have never, in any country, had to give an account of themselves. The Italians have named a Minister of Civil Defense, and in Greece it is the Minister for Public Works who takes the responsibility, but they do hardly any better than our Minister of the Interior. Why does such a situation exist? For many reasons, the most innocent of which is that these ministers find it impossible to perform their jobs correctly. This impossibility results, for example, from the fact that they do not possess the almost absolute authority essential for properly implementing a mobilization as extensive as that which would be required by a large-scale disaster. Although they would find themselves in the midst of a major crisis, they do not have one tenth the authority with which the officials in charge of a general mobilization are invested when they need it.

There are many other causes which still prevent the Minister of the Interior in France, of Public Works in Greece, of Civil Defense in Italy, and their counterparts elsewhere, from operating with acceptable efficiency. They include political mediocrity, the power of pressure groups, and a lack of political courage on the part of certain people who are more concerned about their careers than about the public interest.

Since many of these causes are shared by all the members of a government, it would be best to choose from among them the Minister who is unswayed by at least one of them. And that is the Minister for National Defense, who knows nothing about the paucity of resources that all the other officials complain of. The quantity and quality of the troops which answer only to one person, and the fact that they can be commited to this type of battle would, if the Defense Minister were given that responsibility, be sufficient to make relief work more effective than it is now (provided, of course, that the troops were ones previously trained for that mission, not the usual soldiers that we have all too often seen in too many places around the world providing very little help and even getting in the way in this type of situation).

Moreover, the Minister of Defense commands the armed forces, whose only official mission is to respond to aggression. Whether it comes from a foreign power or from mighty Mother Nature is of little consequence, and therefore there should be no difficulty adding natural threats to those which Defense is already in charge of forestalling.

What is more, whatever the role played in the great battle of post-disaster relief work by civilian entities both public and private, it will always—as it is now with the Minister of the Interior in charge of fighting that battle—be much less important than the role played by military contingents and equipment. Rather than entrusting this very difficult mission to the Interior Minister whose only in-house resources are firefighting forces (which are not obliged to stay in their towns to guarantee the essential safety services that they provide every day) and who will consequently be obliged to ask the Defense Minister to lend some personnel and equipment, why not put the same Defense Minister who already has the necessary personnel and equipment in charge in the first place?

I know how much reluctance, hostility, and rejection would be stirred up by this "revolution" within the microcosm in question, how much it would shock some people and antagonize others. But must we once again sacrifice the general welfare to special interests? Must we knuckle under to lobbying pressure rather than adhere to the ethics of our duties? Must we hide behind our chilly conservatism rather than be boldly innovative and update our timeworn procedures? Must we, as always, do nothing until the next catastrophe forces us to make inescapable reforms? Today these questions and this choice confront every nation on Earth. What was impossible yesterday—protecting ourselves effectively against the risk of earthquakes—is now achievable: earthquakes can be predicted, buildings can be constructed to withstand them, and we could break out of our obsolete, ineffectual habits to organize relief work.

As to what happens after ten days or two weeks—when the rescuers have labored unstintingly, the pseudo-rescuers have tried to draw attention to themselves, the media have scored their scoops, and the intellectual vultures have already taken their positions with their characteristic shrewdness—the result is not always edifying. Although innumerable and generous donations are piling up, although foreign governments have sent substantial assistance in money, in kind, and in various kinds of cooperation, it should be realized that only a minimal fraction of these funds, these supplies, these medications, this equipment, is actually reaching those who escaped death. The more miserable the survivors, the tinier the fraction.

I remember how sickened I was after the terrible earthquake in Chile in 1960. My former occupation as an engineer in the tin mines was still fresh in my memory, and the image that came to me, as I saw the distribution of the millions of dollars sent from all over the world to that country, was of the stacks of sieves used to sort the ore we had extracted before it was sent on for chemical treatment. A half-dozen of these sieves, with finer and finer mesh, divided the run-of-mine ore into categories of decreasing size: on top the "big lumps," which represented almost half the sample in both volume and weight, then the "half-lumps," then the "middlings," then, all the way at the bottom, the "extra-fines." In Chile at that time, I had the impression that a few well-placed politicians, a few high-ranking military officers, a group of business executives and insiders, had gathered up the "big lumps," the "lumps" and the "half-lumps" of the international aid. And at the very bottom of the social scale, all that was left was a mere whiff of the "extra-fines."

I have relived that experience of 1960, I regret to say, in every country, including our own, where each time the misfortune of the many has fattened a rather repugnant minority. That includes long, large, and costly reconstruction programs, and even certain pseudo-scientific or pseudo-humanitarian missions.

BACK TO PREDICTION

"But wait," you will say, "you have told us it is now possible to predict earthquakes: so why are they predicted only in Greece?" And I will answer: because first of all we must overcome the rejection of the VAN method which was the first reaction of most geophysicists in general and seismologists in particular. Some of them—not many, yet—are slowly changing their attitude, but most remain aggressively hostile.

The explanation for this attitude lies, I believe, in a feeling of frustration associated with the fact that Varotsos, Alexopoulos, and Nomikos are not geophysicists, much less seismologists, but two solid-state physicists (V and A) and an electronics engineer (N), and they are thus outsiders in terms of Earth science. That these "outsiders" should have discovered how to predict earthquakes, a result that seismologists could not achieve despite decades of effort, is obviously a difficult thing to forgive. What is more, if this method were to be officially adopted, the funding allocated each year to research in this area might be taken away from them. Two good reasons to reject this heretical intrusion without even examining it.

Since it is difficult to own up to this kind of motivation, others that appear less subjective need to be invented. The insiders have been doing so for eight years– eight years during which they have prevented the political leaders of various countries from adopting the VAN method or even testing it: that means eight more years of continued research funding, and eight more years of keeping up the appearance of their scientific self-respect.

Many criticisms have been levelled against the VAN method by its opponents. The major one is that this method is not based on any theory which explains the genesis of what they refer to as "alleged" precursor signals. I have answered this objection many times, and every time my answer has been in the form of a question: Do you yourself have a proven and exact theory which explains the existence of the Earth's magnetic field and the fact that a magnetized needle always points north? Since the answer to that is "No," I then ask how come, despite this gap in knowledge, the compass has always managed to do what is expected of it for all these years. And I conclude by recalling that for half a century, a majority of geologists denied the fact that the continents drifted around the surface of the globe simply because Wegener—who was not a geologist—could not explain the mechanism.

Mutatis mutandis, the same applies to the VAN method. While waiting for these solid-state physics professors Varotsos and Alexopoulos to explain it—and they themselves will be the first to admit how little they understand the phenomenon at present— it would be stupid, on the basis of dubious academic pretexts, not to make use of the method no matter how empirical it might be. Because it is astonishingly reliable, and it might save millions of lives all over the world each century.

However, pending a physical explanation accepted by everyone, not least of all by the very originators of the method, the serious theoreticians have been thinking about it and formulating hypotheses. Obviously Varotsos and Alexopoulos are doing so, and have published articles on the subject (references to which are listed at the end of this book) in which they present the following idea:

The rocks of the Earth's crust consist of solids; these are crystals which contain microscopic impurities. If we assume that the electrical charge of these impurities is different from the charge on the ions of the crystals that contain them, an interstitial gap which gives rise to a dipole is created, due to charge compensation (that is, electrical neutrality). The orientation of this dipole can change when an ion jumps into this gap. The time required for this dipole to change orientation is called the "relaxation time," and it depends on temperature and pressure. When an external electrical field is present, the dipoles tend to line up parallel to it. However, when temperature and pressure conditions dictate excessively long relaxation times, the dipoles essentially cannot rotate, and thus each one retains the alignment that it had; in other words they do not "feel" the effect of the magnetic field.

But let us assume that while the temperature remains constant, the pressure experienced by the solid progressively increases. This gradual change will lead to a gradual decrease in the relaxation time of the dipoles, and when the pressure reaches a certain critical value, the dipoles will be able to pivot freely and align themselves parallel to the electrical field. This change in polarization will be accompanied by emission of a piezoelectric current, that is, a current associated with a mechanical stress. This is inevitably a transient phenomenon, since the current ceases as soon as all dipoles have aligned themselves with the electrical field.

The genesis of an earthquake can be compared to the phenomenon just discussed. Before the earthquake and in the area where its focus will later be located, stress rises to the critical value at which the dipoles (microinclusions of piezoelectric quartz, for example) align themselves parallel to the external field, and in so doing emit a transient current, the famous "seismic electrical signal," or SES.

But the stresses continue to accumulate, and when they reach the mechanical fracture threshold of the rocks the tremor occurs. This explains the time lapse which separates the SES from the actual quake. This time difference (Δt) is directly proportional to the difference between fracture stress and critical stress, and inversely proportional to the rate at which the stresses in question are increasing.

When I visited Professor Gokhberg, director of the Earth Physics Institute in Moscow, in 1987 and invited him to supplement his research on interpreting the radio precursor signal with a parallel investigation of the SES used in the VAN method, he was not convinced by my arguments. One year later, having witnessed the occurrence of an earthquake predicted by the VAN method, he began thinking about the phenomenon and proposed an explanation for it: based on the dilatancy model, at a given moment during the genesis of an earthquake there may occur, in the area of the future earthquake focus, a compression of the microcrystals in the rocks; when it reaches a value at which interstitial water can be squeezed out, the movements of the liquid would give rise to electromagnetic phenomena causing the SES.

Professor Laurence Slifkin of the University of North Carolina, one of the ten world experts who back in 1984 signed a statement favorable to the VAN method, proposed the following explanation at the international conference on solid-state physics held at Aussois in March 1989: Considering a fault as a linear dislocation, in other words a crystal plane sliding with respect to the adjacent plane, this movement creates a potential difference of several volts between the two ends of the dislocation. At distances of about sixty miles, it is still possible to measure values on the order of a millivolt. This would explain the SES, and would also explain the signals two or three orders of magnitude higher that are recorded in the immediate vicinity of a high-magnitude earthquake (approximately 6 on the Richter scale), such as the one at Kalamata.

SCIENTIFIC CONTROVERSY AND DISHONESTY

Among the usual criticisms is one, still being advanced recently by an official seismologist at the Belgian Royal Observatory at Uccle (Brussels), which states that since Greece is notoriously the most seismically active country in Europe, tremors with a magnitude exceeding 3 on the Richter scale are so numerous there that it is always easy to find one that more or less corresponds to the "alleged" VAN prediction. Even more recently, a statistician has developed the same argument. These are perfect examples of the mental aberration that sometimes permeates our scientific circles: the VAN method in fact takes into account only earthquakes that are potentially destructive and therefore deadly, therefore exceed a magnitude of 4 or more often 4.5; it does not bother with magnitude 3 quakes. Now, approximately 8 to 10 times fewer earthquakes occur for each step up on the magnitude scale; the tremors indicated by the VAN method are thus between 10 times (for magnitude 4) and 1,000 times (for magnitude 6) less numerous than those being discussed by the distinguished Belgian geophysicist and the equally distinguished French mathematician. Moreover the originators of the VAN method have predicted, accurately, a number of tremors with magnitudes exceeding 5 and 6, which are very rare even in Greece. (Let me remind the reader in this connection that the energy of a given number of the Richter scale is almost 33 times greater than the energy of the number just below it.) Moreover, the predictions specify not only the magnitude but also the location of the future epicenter, which demolishes the insinuation that Varotsos was trying to find, *somewhere in Greece* and *after* each of his predictions, an earthquake that would allow him to claim to have predicted it: he predicts in advance both the region where the quake will occur and its magnitude.

Some geophysicists have claimed over the years that Varotsos and his colleagues were not announcing earthquakes *before* the fact but actually *after* the fact. Now that the VAN team is sending its predictions to the government by officially dated telegram (date and time), this argument can no longer be used openly, but all too often it is still implied.

The most virulent enemies of Varotsos are those who, by profession, nationality, or place of residence, are closest to him: certain Greek seismologists first of all, then certain Italian, French, and Belgian geophysicists. Fraternal hatreds are the worst.

On April 4, 1988, Professors J. Drakopoulos, G. Stavrakakis, and L. Latoussakis sent a three-page letter to *Tectonophysics*, from which I have extracted only the following sentences:

"...we also want to draw the attention of the scientific community to the following serious problems. Why do the authors (VAN group) systematically refuse to send their telegrams either to the Government, or to the Seismological Institutes, before the occurrence of a particular earthquake? They mainly just exchange telegrams between themselves (e.g., Mrs. Varotsos-Lazaridou to Professor Alexopoulos)..."

From the reply by Professor Varotsos, dated June 3, 1988, and also three pages long plus two pages of appendices, which appears in the same issue of Tectonophysics, I quote the following lines concerning the accusation made above:

"a) As explained in our previous publication, * until March 18, 1986, our predictions were discussed (before an earthquake occurrence) during sessions of the official Earthquake Prediction Council (EPC) of the Ministry of Public Works. J. Drakopoulos was a member of this Committee, and there are official minutes proving that he signed our predictions before an earthquake occurrence. [We] have published a detailed list of the predictions made during the EPC sessions.*

---

* *Tectonophysics* **152**: 190–193, 1988.

"b) Concerning the M_s = 6.1 earthquake that occurred on March 29, 1986, the pre-seismic information was directly transferred to the Ministry (4 days before the earthquake occurred) as explained by [us].

"c) After April 1986, the Greek Government decided upon the following procedure: before an earthquake occurrence, the prediction (that is, the telegram) should be sent to the Interministerial Committee (IMC) of the Greek Government; this IMC immediately after the receipt of our telegram, sends a copy to the Organization for the Protection from Earthquakes (OASP). J. Drakopoulos is President of the OASP, and hence he is officially informed of our predictions before any tremor. (Two characteristic examples are given in the Appendix of the present paper.)"

I have gone on at some length about this controversy because it illustrates the incredible dishonesty that is sometimes exhibited in a profession—science—in which the highest intellectual rigor ought to be an absolute necessity. But that rigor is too often nonexistent among the careerists, who are too numerous, and among certain others who have already "made it," who are also too numerous. This is what I have called the Lysenko syndrome, which corrupts academia and the research community in France and elsewhere.

Recently, a French geophysicist told the newspaper *Le Figaro* that he was still extremely reticent about the VAN method because its authors did not extensively publish their results and their scientific procedures. "Reticent," in this case, is a euphemism for "hostile." The answer is that people who, lacking the necessary resources (most of all qualified personnel), have to work twelve to sixteen hours a day—to make their network operational, then evaluate miles and miles of chart recordings and, when they find an SES, analyze it, make a diagnosis, and officially alert government representatives—cannot take the time to pursue what, for too many researchers, has become a primary goal: publications rather than research. Varotsos prefers to accumulate results rather than bibliographic citations. Nevertheless, references to his articles, of which he can be proud—and more of their quality than their quantity—are listed at the end of this book.

Too many geophysicists and too many professors opposed the VAN method as soon as it was disclosed. They have opposed it without having seriously studied it and without having discussed it with its creators; they have opposed it *in principle*, the characteristic reflex of every Establishment scientist. Whether religious or political, Establishment thinking is the very antithesis of intelligence. When it comes to religious or political faith, in which rationality is of little or no consequence, such thinking is conceivable if not excusable. But in science...?

Why, you might ask, so much hostility, so much dishonesty, why this Establishment thinking, if you accept my views? Because in the scientific or academic community, this "confraternity" or fraternity, high quality is not very widespread. Nor is generosity towards anyone or anything which might cast a shadow on one's own advancement up the ladder, one's own reputation, one's

129

own self-esteem, or one's research funding. As in any corporation or profession, vanity has its place; even more so since it is considered to be in good taste in this context to appear modest. As far as money is concerned, here as almost everywhere, it reigns abusively supreme.

The funds committed by the industrialized nations to the search for a method of predicting earthquakes are not negligible. The fact that such a method has now been discovered by someone else threatens to dry up one of the sources of your own budget. And that is even more difficult to accept when those discoverers are drawing from the same budgetary well as you are. Hence the decrease with distance in the hostility of the scientists involved: some of their Greek colleagues, as I have said, are the fiercest enemies of the promoters of the VAN method, followed by some of their geographically close European colleagues; but in Moscow I heard almost nothing but constructive criticism, and in Beijing none at all.

I am not talking about conformism, about the intellectual faintheartedness which prevents people from espousing an idea that the scientific and academic establishment has not yet acknowledged. Jules Renard said it best: In order to arrive, first you yourself have to arrive, then the others have to fail to arrive.

This is what is happening with the VAN method. Of all the many scientific figures with whom I have discussed this highly controversial method, it was only in Beijing that I encountered a true and straightforward scientific attitude, summarized in these words: "We will need to investigate the method before taking a position."

What matters in this case is not being right or wrong in some umpteenth little scientific squabble: what matters are human lives. How can we reject a method when almost all of its predictions have been borne out? A method whose only and infrequent failures, which are moreover becoming more and more infrequent as experimental data accumulate, consist in not having predicted 10% of the tremors that have occurred in more than half a dozen years? Such failures are the lot of any new technique, and they are minor when compared to the 90% success rate, especially since they can be explained essentially by the fact that new seismic zone/recording station pairs have not yet been calibrated, and sometimes by a background noise level that drowns out the SES. A method whose predictions have all come true meets astonishingly well the urgent security needs of hundreds of millions of human beings who are threatened by earthquakes This threat very often materializes in regions such as China, Turkey, Greece, Armenia, and the "Ring of Fire" around the Pacific; and much more rarely, but with equally devastating results, in countries like Portugal, Switzerland, France, or the United States.

As I write these lines, in the summer of 1989, I am one of only a few dozen scientists who have taken a definite and even official position in favor of the VAN method. I must be the oldest among them, and that perhaps is one of the reasons why this situation recalls so clearly the plight of the lonely partisans of Wegener's "drift" theory, a few months before the theory of sea floor spreading produced an "overnight" conversion in Wegener's innumerable opponents. I believe that it will not be long before innumerable enemies of the creators of the VAN method will join the ten scientists who, in 1984, signed a statement supporting the method, ten scientists whom I list below in alphabetical order:

Dr. Stuart Crampin of the British Geological Survey;

Prof. Uta Kulhanek, head of the renowned Department of Seismology at the University of Uppsala, Sweden;

Prof. D. Lazarus of the American Physical Society, who teaches physics at the University of Illinois at Urbana;

Prof. Lü Dajiong of the Chinese Academy of Sciences;

Prof. W. Ludwig, director of the Institute of Theoretical Solid State Physics at Münster, Germany;

Dr. Klaus Meyer, a seismologist at Uppsala, Sweden;

Prof. Laurence Slifkin of the University of North Carolina;

Prof. R. Teisseyre of the Polish Academy of Sciences, who teaches seismology at the Institute of Geophysics in Warsaw;

Prof. S. Uyeda, editor in chief of the international journal *Tectonophysics*, published in the United States, and professor of seismology at the Earthquake Research Institute of the University of Tokyo; and

Prof. J. Zschau, director of the Institute of Geophysics in Kiel, West Germany.

Paris, July 25, 1989

BIBLIOGRAPHY

DAVIDOVICI, V., *Génie parasismique* [Earthquake-resistant engineering], Presses de l'École Nationale des Ponts et Chaussées, 1985.

DRAKOPOULOS, J., G. STAVRAKAKIS, and J. LATOUS-SAKIS, "Physical Properties of the Variation of the Electric Field of the Earth preceding Earthquakes–Discussion," *Tectonophysics* **161**:55-57, 1989.

LABEYRIE, J., *La Recherche* **19**:1236–1240 (La Recherche, etc.), 1988.

MEYER, K., P. VAROTSOS, K. ALEXOPOULOS, and K. NOMIKOS, "Efficiency Test of Earthquake Prediction around Thessaloniki from Electrotelluric Precursors," *Tectonophysics* **120**:153–161, 1985.

TAZIEFF, H., *Quand la terre tremble* [When the Earth trembles], Fayard, 1st ed. 1962, rev. and corr. ed. 1986.

VAROTSOS, P. and K. ALEXOPOULOS, "Physical Properties of the Variation of the Electric Field of the Earth preceding Earthquakes I," *Tectonophysics* **110**:73–98, 1984a.

VAROTSOS, P. and K. ALEXOPOULOS, "Physical Properties of the Variation of the Electric Field of the Earth preceding Earthquakes II: Determination of epicenter and magnitude," *Tectonophysics* **110**:99–125, 1984b.

VAROTSOS, P. and K. ALEXOPOULOS, "Stimulated Current Emission in the Earth: Piezostimulated Currents and Related Geophysical Aspects. In *Thermodynamics of Point Defects and Relation with Sulk Properties,*" North-Holland, Amsterdam, pp. 410–412, 417–420, 1986.

VAROTSOS, P., K. ALEXOPOULOS, K. NOMIKOS, and M. LAZARIDOU, "Earthquake Prediction and Electric Signals" *Nature* **322**:120, 1986.

VAROTSOS, P. and K. ALEXOPOULOS, "Physical Properties of the Variation of the Electric Field of the Earth preceding Earthquakes III," *Tectonophysics* **136**:335–339, 1987.

VAROTSOS, P., K. ALEXOPOULOS, K. NOMIKOS, and M. LAZARIDOU, "Official Earthquake Prediction in Greece," in O. Kulhanek (ed.), "Seismic Source Physics and Earthquake Prediction Research," *Tectonophysics* **152**:193–196, 1988.

VAROTSOS, P. and K. ALEXOPOULOS, "Physical properties of the variation of the electric field of the Earth preceding earthquakes—Reply," *Tectonophysics* **161**:58-62, 1989.